Michael J. Bayly
Editor

Creating Safe Environments for LGBT Students
A Catholic Schools Perspective

Pre-publication
REVIEWS,
COMMENTARIES,
EVALUATIONS . . .

"Catholic education has long-needed this worthy resource book for addressing the challenges of increasing numbers of students who identify as lesbian, gay, bisexual, or transgender as well as the rest of the school community who need to be equipped to respond with understanding and compassion. In my experience, teachers and staff are asking for strategies and models of response as well as their justification in Church teaching. *Creating Safe Environments for LGBT Students* is the best and most comprehensive response I have seen. I especially recommend Section 4 for its well-documented presentation on the Church teachings that root this work as a pastoral responsibility and Section 5, which helps us to see this work as the fulfillment of the mission of Catholic education."

Father Jim Schexnayder, MDiv
Resource Director,
National Association of Catholic
Diocesan Lesbian and Gay Ministries

"If you're looking for a Catholic resource that hammers home *only* the Church's official moral teaching about homosexual actions, this is not the resource for you. However, if you're looking for a tool to help create a safe and pastoral environment for LGBT teens, this is an excellent resource. While official Catholic moral teaching is presented clearly and respectfully, there is also ample room here for Catholic social teaching, respect for the inherent and abiding dignity of all, the human sciences, and pastoral care—all grappling with the honest questions LGBT teens really ask. Use the whole program or select what will work in your school setting. It's a multifaceted and sensitively written five session mini-course."

Father Richard Sparks, PhD
Pastor and Moral Theologian

"This book addresses an issue at the frontier of diversity training for Catholic schools. This five session, comprehensive training program is the resource that Catholic schools need to create an environment of dignity and respect for those students who are lesbian, gay, bisexual, and transgender. With its engaging background readings and provocative discussion questions, the training program is tailor-made for raising the consciousness of caring, well-intentioned faculty members who may not be aware of the needs of the LGBT teens in their school. Teachers will be grateful to receive the thoughtful advice offered on such practical matters as how best to support a student who has been harassed, how to present the Church's teaching on human sexuality while still honoring the dignity of every student in the room, and how to respond to speech or behavior which expresses homophobic attitudes. Objections, questions, and concerns that may be raised by members of the school community are addressed in an intelligent and sensitive manner.

The program is truly comprehensive: sessions cover everything from the psychological and theological underpinnings of the program's approach, to school policy, to classroom management and interpersonal boundary-setting. Excellent student skit and prayer service ideas are included, along with an extensive bibliography for further reading.

Fifteen years ago, the USCCB called for educators to offer 'a special degree of pastoral understanding the care' toward youth whose sexual orientation was homosexual. *Creating Safe Environments for LGBT Students* offers the tools that Catholic schools need to respond to that call."

Lorraine Kilmartin
Editor in Chief, Saint Mary's Press

"An excellent resource and a clear call to action. This book is thoughtful and thorough and effectively addresses many levels and aspects of this important work. It challenges the reader and the participants of Safe Staff trainings to be critical thinkers, to have adequate knowledge about GLBT issues, and to be prepared for each level of the work. Readers are reminded to make strong pedagogical connections as they raise GLBT issues in Catholic schools, to understand school policies, and to more deeply investigate and embrace the Catholic social teaching of justice. The book includes clearly articulated directions for those implementing Safe Staff training in their schools and it provides useful and concrete training activities and tools. I especially appreciate how the book includes the courageous voices and moving stories of GLBT youth, and those adults (parents and teachers) who love them. It is gratifying to see that the Safe Staff model that originated in the St. Paul Public School's Out for Equity's Program is being adapted, expanded, and implemented to create safe school climates for GLBT youth in Catholic schools. Having led the charge in 1994 to create Out for Equity, a program serving GLBT students, staff, and families in St. Paul Public Schools, I know firsthand that this work takes courage. A wonderful guide for those who care about our GLBT youth. The book is a testimony to those whose leadership has pushed educators in Catholic education to take a stand for our GLBT youth."

Mary Tinucci, MSW, LICSW
Founder and Coordinator
of Out for Equity; 1996 Recipient
of the Thomas Gumbleton Award
for Outstanding Service to GLBT
Persons in Catholic Education

HPP

Harrington Park Press®
The Trade Division of The Haworth Press, Inc.
New York • London • Oxford

Creating Safe Environments for LGBT Students
A Catholic Schools Perspective

Creating Safe Environments for LGBT Students
A Catholic Schools Perspective

Michael J. Bayly
Editor

Harrington Park Press®
The Trade Division of The Haworth Press, Inc.
New York • London • Oxford

For more information on this book or to order, visit
http://www.haworthpress.com/store/product.asp?sku=5723

or call 1-800-HAWORTH (800-429-6784) in the United States and Canada
or (607) 722-5857 outside the United States and Canada

or contact orders@HaworthPress.com

Published by

Harrington Park Press®, the trade division of The Haworth Press, Inc., 10 Alice Street, Binghamton, NY 13904-1580.

PUBLISHER'S NOTE
The development, preparation, and publication of this work has been undertaken with great care. However, the Publisher, employees, editors, and agents of The Haworth Press are not responsible for any errors contained herein or for consequences that may ensue from use of materials or information contained in this work. The Haworth Press is committed to the dissemination of ideas and information according to the highest standards of intellectual freedom and the free exchange of ideas. Statements made and opinions expressed in this publication do not necessarily reflect the views of the Publisher, Directors, management, or staff of The Haworth Press, Inc., or an endorsement by them.

Identities and circumstances of individuals discussed in this book have been changed to protect confidentiality.

Contents of Handout 1.6 "Recent Research Findings Concerning GLBT Catholic Youth in Catholic Schools" from *Catholic School Facts from GLSEN's National School Climate Surveys,* 2004; and Joseph Kosciw, *The 2003 National School Climate Survey: The School-related Experiences of our Nation's Lesbian, Gay, and Transgender Youth,* 2004 reprinted with permission.

Excerpts quoted from the Congregation for the Doctrine of Faith's 1986 *Letter to the Bishops of the Catholic Church on the Pastoral Care of Homosexual Persons;* 1965 *Declaration on Christian Education;* and *Educational Guidelines in Human Love* (1983) have been reprinted with permission from the Libreria Editrice Vaticana.

Materials from Catholic Pastoral Committee on Sexual Minorities (CPCSM) reprinted with permission.

Excerpts quoted from Anthony Chase, "Violent Reaction: What do Teen Killers Have in Common?" reprinted with permission from *In These Times.*

Excerpts quoted from Thomas J. Gumbleton, "Teaching Authentically," and John R. Quinn, "Toward an Understanding of the Letter on Pastoral Care of Homosexual Persons" reprinted with permission from *America: The National Catholic Weekly.* Visit www.america magazine.org.

"Does It Matter" from Ann Shortall, *In Piecing Together a Caring Community: A Resource Book on Dismantling Homophobia,* reprinted with permission from the Newfoundland-Labrador Human Rights Association.

Quotes from J. O'Leary "Mother Church and Her Gay/Lesbian Children" reprinted with permission from *Ceide.*

Quote from *An Introduction to the Pastoral Care of Homosexual People* reprinted with permission.

Quotes from documents published by the U.S. Conference of Catholic Bishops reprinted with permission.

Cover design by Jennifer M. Gaska.

Library of Congress Cataloging-in-Publication Data

Creating safe environments for LGBT students: A Catholic schools perspective/ Michael J. Bayly, editor.
    p. cm.
Includes bibliographical references and index.
ISBN-13: 978-1-56023-606-1 (soft : alk. Paper)
1. Homosexuality and education–United States. 2. Catholic schools–United States. I. Bayly, Michael J.

LC192.6.C74 2007
371.826'64–dc22

2006016936

This book is gratefully and lovingly dedicated to the late Bill Kummer, CPCSM co-founder, prophetic leader, educator, and advocate for LGBT persons and their families, and to Martin Dohmen, early CPCSM board member, and Bill's loving and dedicated friend, soul mate, and assistant during the early years of CPCSM's Safe Schools Initiative.

During this crucial time in the initiative's history, Bill and Martin tirelessly traveled to each of the eight original participating Catholic high schools to negotiate and organize each school's Safe Staff training program and assemble and orient volunteers. They also spent long hours designing the project's first lesson plans and curriculum materials, which would eventually become the primary source for the first draft of the manuscript for this book.

The idea for CPCSM's Safe Schools Initiative was prompted, in part, by the verbal and physical abuse both Bill and Martin experienced, as gay teenagers, at the hands of their fellow high school students.

Because of their tireless devotion to CPCSM's Safe Schools Initiative, Bill, Martin, and many others have ensured that thousands of present and future LGBT high school students will not only find safer and more welcoming and affirming school environments, but will have a greater chance of leading more satisfying and rewarding lives as contributing LGBT members of both the Church and society.

ABOUT THE EDITOR

Michael J. Bayly, MA, has worked as an educator in Catholic elementary schools, as an adjunct faculty member at the College of St. Catherine in Minneapolis, Minnesota, and as director of the Education for Liberation Program at the Spirit of the Lakes United Church of Christ in Minneapolis. Since 1994, he has worked with the Catholic Pastoral Committee on Sexual Minorities, based in the Twin Cities, most recently serving as the organization's Safe Schools project coordinator and executive coordinator. He also serves as editor of the CPCSM's journal, the *Rainbow Spirit*.

CONTENTS

Foreword

Going deep into complex issues can be frightening and uncomfortable; it can challenge previously held certainties.

Within our Catholic high schools, there are many who view with fear and discomfort not only the increasing number of students who are willing to question and learn about the complex reality of human sexuality, but the willingness of many lesbian, gay, bisexual, and transgender (LGBT) students to claim their sexuality as a positive aspect of their being. It is a tragic fact that many in our society—including our Church and schools—respond to the complex and often uncomfortable reality of sexual diversity with discrimination and violence. Such response, no matter what the context, denies those who are targeted their inherent and precious giftedness as children of God.

The collection of strategies, resources, and insights that you hold in your hands offers creative ways to ensure that the giftedness of LGBT youth is treasured and nurtured within our Catholic high schools. Those who have worked tirelessly over the years to compile the wealth of knowledge and experience contained in these pages have consciously chosen to explore deeply an issue that, at its core, is intrinsically linked to justice-making.

Accordingly, exploring the theology of sexual diversity also involves risk-taking—going forward in faith, trusting that the Spirit will lead, guide, and reveal. It involves openness to the experiences of others and the belief that it is human experience—in all its diversity—that is the only realm available for us within which we can potentially experience the loving and transforming presence and action of God.

Such a disposition compels us to question, challenge, and perhaps revise our understanding of complex human issues once thought to be straightforward and indisputable. This disposition of trust and openness to God incarnate in the lives of all has the potential to inform, challenge, and nourish the Church's theological and doctrinal development. Accordingly, it has the potential to empower individuals and communities toward prophecy.

Prophetic words and deeds shine through this text. And like all prophetic words they speak of justice, inclusiveness, and a vision of the world that is bigger, more encompassing than the one we may be prepared to embrace. Yet, the call to do so remains. It rings forth from these pages—offering a catalyst for transformation.

It is a call, a challenge, that reflects the character of Catholic education, which has a long tradition of aiding and enriching the lives of those who are marginalized–women, immigrants, the poor, the disabled. Our LGBT children comprise yet another group that suffers marginalization, suffers from having its voices silenced, its experiences dismissed. Such treatment is not in accord with either the Good News of our brother Jesus nor the long tradition of Catholic education. I, therefore, believe it crucial that school leaders everywhere—but especially within faith-filled environments—be proactive about the issue of sexual identity and orientation.

The benefits of exploring deeply this issue are numerous: it can be, and has been in some schools, a starting point for introducing and exploring other diversity issues such as racism, classism, sexism, ageism, and ableism. Cultivating deeper understanding and compassion for others who are perceived to be different benefits us all—as individuals and as communities.

To be sure, such efforts will trouble and disturb many. Yet the price to pay for not engaging in this issue is one that is unacceptable. The high suicide rate of LGBT teenagers tells us that this price involves lost lives. It also involves families being torn apart, and individuals and communities experiencing alienation. How can we as Church—as the people of a loving and inclusive God—not respond?

Thomas J. Gumbleton
Auxiliary Bishop, Archdiocese of Detroit (Retired)
October 2005

Preface

In my Creator's house there are many rooms.

John 14:2

The students who comprise our Catholic schools occupy in numerous ways, the "many rooms" that our brother Jesus spoke about. Students who openly identify as lesbian, gay, bisexual or transgender (LGBT) inhabit distinct rooms—sometimes comfortably, sometimes not. They are rooms that are peered into, often fearfully, by other students who are struggling with sexual identity issues and questions. And they are rooms that are an intrinsic and thus potentially sacramental part of God's house, of God's creation. As such they need to be respected and celebrated.

Like all of the Creator's creative spaces, these rooms possess their own loving and transforming light. Human ignorance and fear have cloaked such light for centuries. The interaction promoted in *Creating Safe Environments for LGBT Students: A Catholic Schools Perspective* greatly assists Catholic high school educators in identifying and removing these light-denying cloaks. The removal of oppressive and erroneous barriers is an important component in the building of school communities wherein the welcoming and transforming love of God, our Creator, is clearly discerned within and by all.

Creating Safe Environments for LGBT Students: A Catholic Schools Perspective is, therefore, a unique collection of strategies, resources, experiences, and reflections. It is a collection aimed at encouraging and empowering Catholic high school professionals as they reach out and interact in positive and pastorally sensitive ways with a unique though often invisible population of students.

FIRST STEPS

Like any initiative that seeks to identify the presence of God in human life, the genesis of *Creating Safe Environments for LGBT Students: A Catholic Schools Perspective* can be traced to a very real and dynamic human reality and thus a distinct social and cultural milieu.

In the early-to-mid 1990s there was in the Twin Cities area much talk and publicity around two public school programs—"Out for Equity" in St. Paul, and "Out for Good" in Minneapolis. Both programs sought to address the needs and concerns of LGBT students within their respective school districts. Both were also created and sustained in response to an increasing number of public high school students who were either "coming out"—that is, openly stating that they were bisexual, gay, lesbian, or transgender—or openly exploring questions related to sexual identity and/or orientation.

The Safe Staff framework and model that was developed and used in the Out for Equity Program was particularly instrumental in what would transpire in Catholic education in the Twin

Cities. This model would be adapted, expanded, and implemented in the efforts to create safe school climates for LGBT youth in Catholic schools.

The presence of District 202 in Minneapolis also needs to be acknowledged. It was established in 1993 as the first and only permanent space in Minnesota by and for LGBT youth. District 202 is a unique community brought into being through the vision and proactive efforts of LGBT youth themselves.

In the midst of such topical and—for some—controversial developments, many within the Catholic high school setting began to talk openly of issues related to sexual orientation and youth. Was the phenomenon of an increasing number of students "coming out" in public schools an anomaly? Or was it a wake-up call to the presence of an invisible minority population within their own school communities? What was the authentic Catholic response to such a population? How would such a response impact the wider school community?

In raising and discussing such questions, an informal network of teachers, administrators, school counselors, parents, students, alums, and others began to take shape. Such conversations also brought to light the reality that an increasing number of teachers, counselors, and administrators were being confronted by students in Catholic schools who either identified as LGBT or were struggling with sexual identity/orientation issues. The need for a genuine educational and pastoral response to such students was duly recognized, as was the need to bring the reality of sexual orientation out of the silence and out of the shadows. Yet many within the Catholic educational system felt inadequately prepared to meet such challenges.

A UNIQUE COALITION RESPONDS TO THE CHALLENGE

In 1995, after being approached by teachers, counselors, and administrators requesting training and information regarding the Church's ministry to LGBT persons, the Catholic secondary school presidents of Minneapolis and St. Paul turned to the St. Paul/Minneapolis Archdiocese for guidance. Through the auspices of the Catholic Education and Formation Ministries (CEFM) of the archdiocese, the Catholic Pastoral Committee on Sexual Minorities (CPCSM) was invited to share its long experience and expertise in ministry with LGBT people with both the CEFM and those schools requesting information and training.

CPCSM itself was founded in 1980 and is a grassroots, nonprofit, independent coalition based in the Twin Cities. The group comprises parents, teachers, Catholic School students and alumni, pastoral ministers, and human services professionals—all of various sexual orientations. Much of CPCSM's ministry throughout the 1980s and early 1990s was focused on educational and advocacy activities aimed at encouraging parishes to be welcoming and supportive places for LGBT people.

CPCSM's ministry has always been inspired by a zeal for inclusive justice and a passion for embracing diversity—especially as it relates to issues of sexual orientation and identity. The group firmly believes that members of sexual minorities, by virtue of their struggle to maintain a sense of personal integrity and authenticity, have unique gifts to offer the Church and society. Accordingly, like numerous progressive Catholic organizations and communities, CPCSM operates with the understanding that one's sexuality can and must be affirmed as a gift and as an essential element to be integrated holistically into one's faith life. Reflecting this, CPCSM's Mission Statement reads as follows: "We pledge to create just and safe environments within the Catholic Church and society in which the dignity and integrity of gay, lesbian, bisexual and transgender (GLBT) persons and their families are recognized and affirmed."

Resonating with the theological and pastoral underpinnings of this statement and committed to the ultimate goal of such a mission, the secondary school presidents chose to continue in dialogue with both CPCSM and CEFM. A series of diocesan-wide workshops resulted—planned and implemented with input from CPCSM. These workshops were open to all interested persons and were aimed at providing a general introduction to LGBT concerns within the context of Catholic education.

This period of dialogue was followed in October 1996 by a call from the secondary school presidents for the establishment of an Archdiocesan Study Group on Pastoral Care and Sexual Identity Issues. This group, comprising representatives from each of the involved schools as well as representatives from both CEFM and CPCSM, worked to identify and prioritize the needs of LGBT students and to determine the most appropriate and effective strategies and resources to address these needs. The most fundamental need recognized was for comprehensive training to enable Catholic educators to deal with LGBT youth in a pastorally sensitive and nonjudgmental manner.

SAFE STAFF TRAINING

In response to the findings of the Archdiocesan Study Group on Pastoral Care and Sexual Identity Issues, CPCSM spearheaded the Safe Schools Initiative—an initiative already underway in an informal capacity at a number of Catholic high schools in the archdiocese. From 1997 to 1999, the Safe Schools Initiative involved members of CPCSM planning and facilitating fourteen four-session sequences of comprehensive training at seven archdiocesan high schools—resulting in 275 faculty and staff being trained as "safe staff." Throughout, the training program was adapted, refined, and open to ongoing evaluation by both trainers and trainees.

A crucial component of the Safe Schools Initiative involved supporting faculty in understanding the range of Catholic teaching pertaining to both human sexuality and social justice. The training.also involved ways of promoting such teaching in the classroom in pastorally sensitive, nonjudgmental ways.

Some of the topics covered by the Safe Schools Initiative included: "LGBT Youth: Stages of Coming Out," "Safe Staff: Definitions, Qualities, Roles & Responsibilities," "Your Classroom," "Safe School Environment," "Adapting School Policies," "Supporting Each Other as Safe Staff," "School Climate and Reducing Homophobia," "Guidelines for Responding to Youth" and "Knowing and Developing Resources." In some cases, the topics addressed had never before been considered as "training exercise" material, for example, "Pastoral Care Situations *Vis-a-Vis* Church Teaching" and "Professional Relationship and Boundary Issues."

The Safe Schools Initiative employed a range of both didactic and experiential strategies— role-play and practice scenarios, formal presentations, videos, and question and comments sessions. Each training session began with a LGBT-focused prayer and/or reflection. Some of these prayers, along with the numerous strategies, exercises, and resources, are included in *Creating Safe Environments for LGBT Students: A Catholic Schools Perspective,* as have reflections and insights from teachers, administrators, parents, and students whose lives have been positively and powerfully impacted by the Safe Schools Initiative. The inclusion of such material ensures that *Creating Safe Environments for LGBT Students: A Catholic Schools Perspective* not only serves as a valuable educational resource, but as a historical record and faith-testimony of the many and varied individuals and communities involved.

It is also important to acknowledge the effects that the Safe Schools Initiative has had on other areas of school life. The training forum was the impetus for diversity initiatives on racism and classism that were subsequently implemented in some Catholic high schools. Partly as a result of the positive ends achieved by Safe Schools Initiative, a groundbreaking 1998 meeting of Catholic high school boards recognized and highlighted the importance of LGBT students and the issues that confront them.

One further result of the Safe Schools Initiative is that it has empowered individual teachers and students to develop and implement initiatives of their own. Within particular Catholic high schools, for instance, editorial collectives promoting greater representation of LGBT issues in school newspapers and expanded and updated LGBT media resources are now operative. The equivalent to a "Gay-Straight Alliance" operates in one of the high schools.

BACKLASH

Not all consider the concept of safe staff training as one that should be integrated into our Catholic schools. In the mid-1990s, for instance, local conservatives formed a specific organization to undermine the Safe Schools Initiative. This group and others view such an initiative as "invading school curriculum" with "teachings contrary to Church teaching." Sadly, such groups fail to recognize or acknowledge the pastoral and social justice grounding of safe staff training. Instead, such training is seen to be "instructing administrators, teachers, librarians and counselors [in] how to promote the GLBT agenda" (letter to the editor of the *St. Paul Pioneer Press,* July 19, 2003). This "agenda," however, is never actually spelt out by such conservative groups who seem unresponsive to the movement of the Spirit in and through the lives of those whose experiences take them beyond what has been narrowly defined as orthodox. Regardless, this vocal minority has had a chilling effect on safe staff training initiatives within many schools, and has effectively halted CPCSM representatives from being active participants in any training that does take place.

Yet such a pastoral initiative is not dependent on any outside organization. Many of the schools originally involved in the Safe Schools Initiative have continued and expanded the initiative with yesterday's first wave of trainees becoming today's trainers of their peers.

THE JOURNEY CONTINUES . . .

CPCSM firmly believes that the need for greater awareness and education regarding the issue of LGBT youth and Catholic education—a need clearly demonstrated and responded to within the St. Paul/Minneapolis Archdiocese—is, in fact, a nationwide need. The compilation of *Creating Safe Environments for LGBT Students: A Catholic Schools Perspective* was the first phase toward sharing nationwide CPCSM's wealth of strategies and resources that have been proven to be genuinely innovative, pastoral, and empowering for educators, parents, and students.

CPCSM's work relating to the vision of *Creating Safe Environments for LGBT Students: A Catholic Schools Perspective* has ensured that the organization has received national recognition. In 1999, CPCSM was awarded the Mission Award for Non-Profit Advocacy by the Minnesota Council of Non-Profits. Also, in July 2000, CEFM received the prestigious 2000 SPICE (Selected Programs for Improving Catholic Education) Award from the National Catholic Education Association for integrating the social teachings of the Church into Catholic education. This award was given, in large part, as a result of the groundbreaking safe staff training model put into place by CPCSM while working with CEFM.

The word about *Creating Safe Environments for LGBT Students: A Catholic Schools Perspective* is definitely out, and has engendered much interest and enthusiasm. Furthermore, as we continue our ministry with and for the LGBT community, CPCSM continue to hear the stories of people's high school experiences and what a positive difference a resource like *Creating Safe Environments for LGBT Students: A Catholic Schools Perspective* would have had on their lives at that time and beyond.

Clearly, the time for *Creating Safe Environments for LGBT Students: A Catholic Schools Perspective* has arrived.

Introduction

Creating Safe Environments for LGBT Students: A Catholic Schools Perspective has come at an important time in the history of Catholic schools. For today, a crisis exists among students in the Catholic school who are lesbian, gay, bisexual, or, transgendered (LGBT). While some might argue that this crisis is based on confusion or ignorance about the Roman Catholic Church's teaching on homosexuality, I believe it is not. The Church's teachings are clear and comprehensible to students and adults alike. Rather, the crisis for LGBT students is a fundamentally spiritual one: How is it that I am made in the image and likeness of God and thus inherently dignified, while at the same time I am (in the language of the Vatican) "intrinsically disordered"?

With so much attention on the regulation of homosexual behavior, too little attention has been given to listening to the pain that is in the human heart oriented toward human connection. Moral instruction alone compounds LGBT students' crisis of alienation, meaninglessness and, in some cases, the impossibility of hope. If the pain they feel as they struggle with human connection is to be carefully heard and fully responded to, moral instruction must always have a consistent emphasis on the *imago dei*—the image of God—within, and thus the continual promotion of the dignity of every student. Finally, moral instruction must also be accompanied by direct action that guarantees a learning environment that is free of all forms of hate, hostility, invisibility, and harassment. *Creating Safe Environments for LGBT Students: A Catholic Schools Perspective* thus seeks to engage its participants to be compassionate, knowledgeable, and supportive for all students in the Catholic schools.

The richness of our Roman Catholic tradition teaches that every human being is created in the image and likeness of God, and for that reason deserves respect and dignity. Dignified and respected, this image is reflected in a human sexuality that encompasses the transcendent capacity of every human being to connect with other human beings in many and varied levels of intimacy. Ultimately this transcendence is the capacity for God and the vehicle through which one strives for holiness. It is pervasive in every human being and operative in every human connection to persons and things. Moreover, human sexuality is more than physical sexual acts.

Perhaps a brief reflection can explore these ideas further. For the next few moments, reflect on the environment in which you live or work. Consider the space itself: the absence or presence of a desk, tables, student desks, chairs, shelves, books, pictures, photos, computer, filing cabinet, and so on. As you visualize this space, identify objects or articles that might reveal your sexuality to someone observing it. Then imagine putting each of these items away; put away photos, sayings, symbols, and pictures, any clues that might reveal your human connections.

Reflect further on a typical Monday conversation with colleagues. You are asked about your weekend activities, projects around the home, social obligations, etc. Again, review that weekend and eliminate any reference whatever to people and events that might reveal to your listener your human sexuality. Simply note each of these conversations and restate these activities without references to who you are connected to in life.

By participating in this brief reflection, you may have realized that the attempt to remove clues of your own human sexuality is a challenge that requires unbelievable effort. Both consciously and unconsciously, people continually present clues to whom and toward what they are oriented. In fact, the ability to completely eliminate these clues is impossible. For some readers, the sug-

Creating Safe Environments for LGBT Students
© 2007 by The Haworth Press, Inc. All rights reserved.
doi:10.1300/5723_01

1

gestion to remove these clues brings up feelings of sadness, because in and at work there are many subtle and not-so-subtle clues about who they love and with whom they enjoy life. In this reflection they realize how much love affirms and supports who they are with others. And perhaps most importantly, this basic orientation toward life is the context within which they teach and minister. For other readers who have just read this reflection, they may have had no clues to put away because they have never put them out. A high degree of invisibility is their way of life every day. It is important to remember that as this situation can be the experience of adults, it is also the experience of some of our students.

Perhaps too a story can highlight the constitutive element of the dignity of all persons and the beauty of human sexuality found throughout Catholic teaching. During the Civil Rights Movement of the 1960s, the Student Non-Violent Coordinating Committee conducted voter registration for blacks in the South. Commonly referred to as SNCC (and pronounced *snic*), their nonviolent resistance and voter registration program was in response to a very basic question: Does the Constitution of the United States apply to every citizen or not? SNCC emphasized that if the Constitution did not apply to every citizen, then it needed to be amended to say that it did not. But if it did apply to all Americans, then it applied to the African Americans, and each had the right to vote. Thus, SNCC organized voter registration because it was a constitutional right. Today, thirty-five years later, such a daring act goes unnoticed and unchallenged, that is, every American citizen, eighteen years and older, can vote. Yet the passing of time can be deceptive: many young people during the Civil Rights Movement, who were between fifteen and twenty-five years old, not only suffered brutality, but also lost their lives in the cause of desegregation and the right to vote. These blatant acts of violence against SNCC members occurred because registering and voting by African Americans contained significant social and political implications.

I was reminded of that part of Civil Rights history when, several years ago, after presenting the Roman Catholic Church's teaching on homosexuality, a student at my Catholic high school remained after class. With utmost respect and sincerity, she stated that she was bisexual and then asked a similarly fundamental question of me, her teacher and campus minister, and, perhaps, in her estimation, a representative of the Roman Catholic Church: "Am I created in God's image and likeness? Am I deserving of respect, safety, and support?" Since that time a number of students have broken silence and asked to become visible at my high school. LGBT youth want to learn in an environment that is neither hostile, harassing, nor negating the value of who they are.

Note well: these disclosures do not arise from an environment that does not make clear the church's teaching on homosexuality. Rather, it has been when this teaching has been presented that students have spoken and questioned whether or not they are made in God's image and likeness, and whether or not they are deserving of dignity, respect, safety, and support. Through the voices of these students, God is calling us to listen and to conduct not only ourselves but also our classrooms and schools as the embodiment of compassion and respect, safety, and support.

You hold in your hands a thoughtful and thorough means to learning about and responding compassionately to LGBT students in your school. But you also hold something more: an opportunity for your own ongoing personal transformation. We live in a time where general concern usually arises when teaching human sexuality to adolescents. These concerns and sometimes outright opposition surface when including gay, lesbian, bisexual, and transgendered persons within the realm of human sexuality.

As you use the strategies and resources that comprise *Creating Safe Environments for LGBT Students: A Catholic Schools Perspective,* engage both your mind and heart. Navigating through the chapters of this manual, you are invited to set sail and trust. Put your trust in God's grace within the transforming process of learning what is contained therein. Start employing the concepts of "both/and" rather than "either/or." That is to say, a Catholic school can *both* present the Church's teaching on homosexuality *and* respect, support and provide a safe environment for students who are LGBT. In other words, *the moral teachings on homosexuality* (published in

1986 and 1992 documents by the Congregation for the Doctrine of the Faith and subsequently in *The Catechism of the Catholic Church*), need not be compromised by programs that provide pastoral care to all students. Rather, these moral teachings need to be taught and understood within the broader context of the social teachings of the Church. That is to say, the particular directives regarding homosexual behavior do not supercede the fundamental social teaching that all are created in the image and likeness of God and are entitled to basic human rights, while also having the responsibility to ensure that others' rights are respected.

Genevieve Goodsil-Todd
October 2005

Suggestions for Using this Resource

The safe staff training manual, *Creating Safe Environments for LGBT Students: A Catholic Schools Perspective,* grew out of a series of safe staff training workshops developed and implemented in the mid-late 1990s by the Catholic Pastoral Committee on Sexual Minorities (CPCSM).

The strategies, resources, and reflections that comprised this training have been updated and arranged into five two-hour sessions so as to form a comprehensive manual that not only focuses on classroom initiatives but on longer-term ones as well, such as school policy development. When initiated by Catholic high school professionals, these initiatives can help create and maintain environments of respect, safety, and support for all students—though in particular, those who struggle with questions and issues related to sexual orientation and identity.

It's important to note that the term "safe staff" is problematic for some as it implies that those who have not been formally trained are unsafe. In some schools, alternative names have been devised. One Catholic high school in Minnesota, for instance, chose the term "anchor staff" and the symbol of the anchor to represent themselves. The anchor was chosen as it is one of the earliest Christian symbols and represents faith and stability. The faculty and staff in that particular school who identify as Anchor Staff, believe in the giftedness of LGBT students in their totality. Such belief leads to stability and safety for all students, and a recognition that the life and teaching of Jesus—grounded in radical inclusiveness and justice—represent the ultimate anchor.

The program offered by this manual is by no means definitive. Knowledge and awareness of issues related to LGBT youth and human sexuality continues to expand. Those who utilize this program are encouraged to supplement it with these new insights along with their own and others' personal stories, prayers, and reflections.

The Lasallian educational principles derived from St. John the Baptist De LaSalle, a French priest in the 1600s and founder of the Christian Brothers, comprise key fundamentals in the development of *Creating Safe Environments for LGBT Students: A Catholic Schools Perspective.* De LaSalle revolutionized education in his time by bringing together rich and poor children in the same classroom and by training teachers to open the hearts and minds of a diverse group of students. As a result of his work, St. John the Baptist De LaSalle is recognized by the Catholic Church as the Patron Saint of Teachers. The Lasallian principles encourage faith, service, community, diversity, and justice education. These same principles are reflected in and promoted by *Creating Safe Environments for LGBT Students: A Catholic Schools Perspective.*

In offering *Creating Safe Environments for LGBT Students: A Catholic Schools Perspective* to the faculty and staff of a Catholic high school, a core group of teachers is needed to assume the program's role of "facilitator." This facilitation introduces the program's key topics and the facilitator guides colleagues in reviewing, discussing, and role-playing the various ideas, strategies, and resources presented in each of the five sessions.

It's important to note that the five-session structure is not mandatory. Those serving collectively as "the facilitator," are encouraged to shape and restructure the content of this program so as to accommodate the schedules of as many faculty/staff members as possible. Thus the pro-

Creating Safe Environments for LGBT Students
© 2007 by The Haworth Press, Inc. All rights reserved.
doi:10.1300/5723_02

gram could be offered as an all-day staff development initiative or stretched out over a semester in ten one-hour sessions.

Those serving as program facilitators (and ideally they should number at least two) need to prepare for the role by becoming familiar not only with the program's content, but with as much as possible of the material to which the manual directs by way of its bibliography. In electing to serve in this role, these individuals are demonstrating leadership ability within their school communities, displaying a passion for embracing diversity concerns and a willingness to lead their peers in a journey of discovery and empowerment for the sake of all the students in their care.

For additional preparation and information, those desiring to facilitate safe school initiatives in their school communities are welcomed to visit the Web site of the Catholic Pastoral Committee on Sexual Minorities at www.cpcsm.org.

For some Catholic educators, implementing a safe schools program in their communities will not be possible at present. There is, undoubtedly, a backlash against such initiatives in many dioceses and communities. Nevertheless, individual teachers can and should take and implement what they can from the *Creating Safe Environments for LGBT Students: A Catholic Schools Perspective* program—one that contains a range of both didactic and experiential strategies.

The manual also gathers reflections and insights from teachers, parents, and students whose lives have been positively impacted by Safe School initiatives. Accordingly, *Creating Safe Environments for LGBT Students: A Catholic Schools Perspective* not only comprises a valuable educational resource, but a historical record and faith testimony of the ongoing work of many within Catholic education dedicated to ensuring that the Gospel message of God's inclusive and transforming love is recognized and experienced by all within our Catholic schools.

A NOTE ABOUT THE ROLE-PLAY ACTIVITIES

Role-plays can be an effective way of thinking through and practicing potential situations. The role-plays contained in *Creating Safe Environments for LGBT Students: A Catholic Schools Perspective* touch upon several aspects of creating and maintaining safe environments for youth—especially LGBT youth.

Each role-play exercise addresses one or more of the following aspects of Catholic high school life:

- *Pedagogy:* Making curriculum decisions and designing ways of teaching for greater inclusivity and respect for diversity.
- *Personal Places:* Identifying the teacher/staff person's own level of knowledge and comfort.
- *Pastoral Care:* Providing support to the LGBT or questioning student within the framework of Catholic teaching.
- *Policy and Procedure:* Designing step-by-step action plans that involve administrative decisions (i.e., school policy).

When approaching any of the role-play activities, first seek to identify to which of these four aspects it relates. Then reflect on your action plan—including use of language—for this particular situation. Remember, there is no absolute or "correct" way of responding in every situation. Allow the role-play activities to generate discussion along with formulation of strategies.

Session 1

Laying the Foundations

I believe that there is a crisis among LGBT youths in Catholic schools today.

This crisis is not the result of being LGBT, but rather of hearing only moral instruction on homosexuality with little to no pastoral response. This crisis provides all of us as members of the Body of Christ, with the opportunity to provide respectful, supportive, and safe schools for all students. Such courageous action is more than meeting the needs of the times. It is a way of embodying the timeless mandate of the Gospel of Jesus.

Catholic High School Teacher

Topics Explored

- The crisis facing LGBT youths in our Catholic schools.
- Recognizing the "pervasive presence" of human sexuality.
- Acknowledging the role of our "cultural context" in shaping our understanding of LGBT issues.
- Common fallacies and stereotypes of LGBT persons.
- LGBT terms and definitions.
- Recent research findings concerning LGBT youths in Catholic schools.
- Psychosocial aspects of LGBT youths.
- Understanding sexual identity and orientation.
- A framework for discussing the LGBT reality within the context of Catholic education.

Recommended Equipment/Resources

Name tags
Easel with pad and markers
Notepads, pens, and pencils
Prayer: "Does It Matter?" (see Appendix 1)

Handouts

1.1   A Teacher Reflects on the Crisis in Catholic Schools
1.2   A Reflection on Human Sexuality
1.3   Common Fallacies and Stereotypes of LGBT People
1.4   Human Sexuality Definitions
1.5   LGBT Youths: Some Basic Pastoral Assumptions

Format

1. Facilitator begins Session 1 by sharing the first three verses of a reflection written anonymously by a gay teenager and titled "Does It Matter?" (see Appendix 1).

2. Facilitator distributes Handout 1.1 "A Teacher Reflects on the Crisis in Catholic Schools" to participants and notes that this initial training session and the four that will follow have been designed to respond to the crisis that is identified by the author of Handout 1.1 and powerfully expressed in the reflection by the anonymous gay youths who wrote "Does It Matter?" Throughout the four sessions of this Safe Staff Training, participants will gain and share information about the gay, lesbian, bisexual, and transgender (LGBT) reality and explore ways by which as members of a Catholic high school, they can provide respectful, supportive, and safe schools for all students.

3. Facilitator elicits thoughts and responses from participants regarding Handout 1.1.

4. The facilitator outlines the objectives of this first foundational session and emphasizes that the material to be covered comprises a broad but valuable overview in beginning to understand the reality and specific concerns and needs of LGBT youths and of youths struggling with sexual identity/orientation issues. The facilitator may also wish to note that much of what brings people together for this and for future Safe Staff Training sessions is a deep longing to reach out to all students in their care, but especially to those who, because of issues regarding sexual identity and orientation, may feel themselves to be unreachable.

5. Facilitator notes that in establishing a classroom of respect, safety, and support, it is vital that the teacher has developed an acceptance of his or her own sexuality. Participants read and discuss Handout 1.2 "A Reflection on Human Sexuality," written by a Catholic high school teacher and based on her observations.

6. Facilitator notes that throughout the four Safe Staff Training sessions, human sexuality will be understood as meaning more than physical sexual acts. Instead, it will be understood as encompassing the transcendent capacity of every human to connect with other human beings in many varied levels of intimacy. The following brief guided reflection is shared so as to demonstrate human sexuality defined in this way and to affirm and/or develop sensibilities about sexual identity/orientation.

A Guided Reflection: The Pervasive Presence of Human Sexuality

For the next few minutes, I invite you to reflect on the environment in which you work or live. Consider the space itself–the presence or absence of such things as your desk, tables, student desks, chairs, shelves, books, pictures, photos, computer, filing cabinet, etc. For just a few moments, examine this space and remove any articles from it that might reveal your sexuality to someone observing it. Put away photos, sayings, symbols, and pictures, any "clues" that might reveal toward whom you are attracted and with whom you are connected in life. Simply note each of these items and then put them away.

Reflect further on a typical Monday conversation with colleagues. You are asked about your weekend activities, projects around the home, social obligations, etc. Here again, review that weekend and eliminate any reference whatsoever to people and events that might reveal to your listener your sexuality. Simply note each of these conversations and imagine what it would be like to attempt to recount your weekend activities without references toward who you are connected in life.

7. Facilitator observes that although this reflection is brief, the attempt to remove "clues" of one's human sexuality is a challenge requiring unbelievable effort. Both consciously and unconsciously, people continually present clues to whom and why they are oriented. In fact, the ability to completely eliminate these clues is impossible to achieve. It is not uncommon to feel a certain degree of sadness when we mentally remove these clues. There are, after all, many subtle and not-so-subtle clues in the workplace about who we love and with whom we enjoy life. During this reflection we may be reminded how much love affirms and supports who we are with others.

For some, however, there may be no "clues" to put away as they were never put out in the first place. This can be the case for many LGBT people where a certain degree of invisibility comprises their everyday way of life. It is important to remember that as this situation can be the experience of adults, it also can be the experience of some of our students. Indeed, LGBT youths comprise an often invisible minority in our schools.

8. Facilitator reminds participants that as teachers they need to be cognizant of their own cultural context when they first learned about homosexuality. That initial context may still influence how they may respond to students with regard to LGBT issues.

As an exercise to explore "cultural context," the facilitator writes the following words either on a whiteboard or on large sheets of paper taped to the walls: "Gay," "Lesbian," "Bisexual," and "Transgender." The facilitator asks the participants to think back to their earliest notions, images, and perceptions about these four terms and to honestly share with the group what these were—regardless of whether such images and perceptions were positive or negative, whether such images were based upon facts or stereotypes.

All responses offered by participants are recorded under the appropriate term. A brief discussion follows concerning where and how such images and perceptions were formulated.

Some guiding questions may include the following:

- How old were you when you first heard these terms?
- When and how did you first became aware of the reality of homosexuality?
- Who was present? What happened? What was said?
- What sustained these images and perceptions?
- What eventually challenged them?

Emphasize that much of our earliest information about the issue of homosexuality was in fact comprised of harmful fallacies and stereotypes.

9. Participants view and discuss Handout 1.3 "Some Common Fallacies and Stereotypes of LGBT Persons." In response to participants' specific questions, facilitator may refer to information in Appendix 2 "Countering Common Fallacies and Stereotypes of LGBT Persons."

10. Handout 1.4 "Human Sexuality Definitions" is distributed. Facilitator notes that language is a dynamic, changing reality. This is particularly true with the language of diversity and the terms ("labels") we use to identify ourselves. At all times we must guard against allowing the language we use to demean, exclude, or offend. We must allow others to self identify, as definitions of terms will vary for everyone. The definitions contained in Handout 2.5 are given to provide a starting point for discussion and understanding. Although the facilitator may choose to highlight certain terms and definitions, this handout is primarily designed as a resource for future use rather than an in-class opportunity for lengthy discussion.

11. Participants view and discuss Handout 1.5 "LGBT Youths: Some Basic Pastoral Assumptions." Note that these important assumptions are undermined by fallacies and stereotypes.

12. Participants view and discuss Handout 1.6 "Recent Research Findings Concerning LGBT Youths in Catholic Schools." Facilitator notes that these findings are provided by the Gay and Lesbian and Straight Education Network (www.glsen.org)—a national organization founded in 1993 and dedicated to ensuring safe and effective schools for all students. More information about GLSEN—including its history—will be provided in Session 5 "The Classroom Setting and Beyond." Facilitator also notes that further research findings concerning LGBT youths will be shared in Session 3 "Coming Out."

13. Participants view and discuss Handout 1.7. "Important Points Concerning Psycho-Social Aspects of LGBT Youths."

14. Facilitator notes that the name Kinsey crops up frequently when the issue of sexual orientation or identity is discussed and when statistical information regarding homosexuality is presented. Therefore, it is important to have some rudimentary knowledge of Alfred Kinsey and his research work.

- *Biographical Notes:* Alfred Kinsey (1894-1956) published *Sexual Behavior in the Human Male* in two volumes in 1948 and 1952. In 1953, Kinsey and his colleagues published *Sexual Behavior in the Human Female.* These works are often referred to as the Kinsey Report and remain to date the largest and most significant study of human sexuality. Another study by Alan Bell, Martin Weinberg, and Susan Hammersmith, titled *Sexual Preference: Its Development in Men and Women,* was published in 1982. Both this study and the Kinsey Report were conducted under the auspices of the Alfred C. Kinsey Institute for Sex Research at the University of Indiana in Bloomington, Indiana. Both meet the criteria of legitimate research.

- *Kinsey's Work:* Through the development of a seven-point rating scale based on research findings, the Kinsey Report was the first scientific study to reveal the rich variety of human sexual expression.

- *The Kinsey Scale,* also known as the continuum of sexual orientation, has a range of zero to six. The zero category includes all people who are exclusively heterosexual and report no homosexual experience or romantic and/or sexual fantasies. Category six includes those who are exclusively homosexual in experience and romantic and/or sexual fantasies. Everyone else falls somewhere in between.

15. Using Handout 1.8, the facilitator shares and encourages discussion around some of Kinsey's findings.

- *An Update Regarding the 1948 Kinsey Study on Males:* In 1979, the authors of *The Kinsey Data* (Gebhard et al., 1979) reanalyzed the original data, eliminating prisoners and volunteers from groups with known sexual bias, such as gay organizations. This recalculation revealed that 9.9 percent of college-educated white males and 12.7 percent of those with less than a college education were more or less exclusively homosexual for at least three years (between the ages of sixteen and fifty-five) and 34 percent of all males had experienced some homosexual experience (almost identical with original findings).

- *The Concept of "Homosexualities:"* In 1986, the Kinsey Institute held a symposium for researchers from many varied fields—anthropology, psychology, biology, history, medicine, psychiatry, and sociology—which reexamined the issue of sexual orientation and assessed the usefulness of the Kinsey Scale. In *Homosexuality: Opposing Viewpoints,* editors David Bender and Bruno Leone note that the symposium, published as the book *Homosexuality/Heterosexuality: Concepts of Sexual Orientation,* was "notable for the conclusions that were *not* drawn." For instance, the researchers unanimously challenged the idea, upon which the original scale had been based, that sex acts per se measured sexual orientation. Instead, they agreed that the behavioral scale—measuring the sexual acts a person engages in—had to be balanced with other scales measuring love, sexual attraction, fantasy, and self-identification—all of which could change over time. There is probably no essential heterosexual or homosexual nature, but many "homosexualities" and "heterosexualities" that characterize people. In other words, according to their report, sexual orientation is "multidimensional, situational, changeable, contextual."

16. Facilitator notes that to conclude Session 1, the interrelated issues of official church teaching, pastoral care, and sexual orientation will be discussed and explored. To begin this exploration, the facilitator poses the following question to participants and elicits their response: "On what theological basis can and ought any Catholic school provide pastoral care to students with concerns about sexual orientation?"

Facilitator notes that this crucial question can be addressed by considering (1) a theological presupposition that sexual orientation is a basic orientation toward relationship, and (2) a composite of four continuums reflecting four aspects of human identity. Handouts 1.11 and 1.12 are viewed and discussed by participants.

17. Content of Handouts 1.11 and 1.12 can be summarized by the facilitator through the following summary remarks:

- Sexual identity constitutes a fundamental orientation toward others. As is noted on the continuums, it involves more than behavior. Sexual identity is the manner in which people are in relation to everyone, that is, their manner of being in the world.

- In this way, sexual identity is understood on the level of ontology and not volition. That is to say, as pastoral care is given to the student who discern who he or she is in relation to others, sexual identity is understood as a way of being in the world; it is a discovery on an ontological level. How an individual chooses to behave and live from that basic identity is a function of prayerful discernment and personal conscience.

- Therefore, any focus on pastoral care must include more than church teaching that restricts behavior. While remaining mindful and respectful of these teachings, emphasis must also be placed on the whole student as a spiritual being who is oriented toward God. In addition, the way in which students experience love—from their pastoral care providers, teachers, family, and friends—must always be understood as a participation in the love and care of God.

- Because Catholic teachings have consistently pronounced that sexual orientations other than heterosexuality are disordered and incapable of reflecting the unconditional love of God, serious psychological and spiritual ramifications for youths growing in faith must be anticipated.

18. In light of these summary remarks, the facilitator observes that the pastoral care for students with questions concerning sexual identity/orientation is a matter of justice and spiritual development. To stress this observation the following is shared:

- In general, Catholic social teaching emphasizes that every human being's *right* to life, food, shelter, health care, employment, and education is every other person's *duty*. That is to say, each student's right to education is the teacher's obligation to provide a safe and supportive environment so that learning can take place.

- A broader understanding of sexual identity as a way of being in relation to others and ultimately toward God can support students who are gay, lesbian, bisexual, or transgender, and contribute to a school environment that is both respectful, inclusive, and free from harassment and invisibility. In this way, a safe and supportive environment for learning is a matter of justice. It is hoped that efforts to make the Catholic school respectful of all people will be a modeling of a love that can be a nurturing context for every student's encounter with the immense and unconditional love of God.

19. Facilitator elicits comments and questions in response to Handout 1.11 "A Reflection on the Ongoing Development of Church Doctrine."

20. Facilitator notes that in Session 4 The LGBT Reality and the Catholic Church, a comprehensive overview of the ongoing development of official church teachings regarding sexual

orientation will be presented. The following points, however, are essential for establishing an informed framework for any presentation on this topic:

- No discussion on the Church's developing understanding and teaching on sexual orientation can take place outside the broader context of the Church's understanding of human sexuality.
- Much of the understanding of human sexuality articulated by the Catholic Church today can be traced back to a limited understanding of human anatomy that was held by past generations. The Church teaches that every sex act must be open to the possibility of procreation and must occur within the context of Christian marriage between a male and female. This teaching has its roots in the era of human history and scientific understanding when the male was considered to hold and transmit life via the "sacred seed." Both science and the Church at that time were ignorant of the role that the female plays in the procreative process. The female was viewed solely as an incubator for the "sacred seed" that was deposited by the male during sexual intercourse. Thus in the Old Testament scriptures, and later in the writings of St. Thomas Aquinas, masturbation was considered a greater sin than incest or rape, as at least in the case of the latter, the "seed," containing human life, was deposited within a female where it could grow, as opposed to being "spilled" outside where it would die.
- For centuries the Church viewed the gift of human sexuality and, in particular, female sexuality with suspicion. Females, because of the natural processes of menstruation and childbearing, were more readily equated with "nature," traditionally understood as "fallen," and thus chaotic and dangerous. Men, on the other hand, because of their perceived ability to transmit human life, were understood to be closer to reason (and thus human culture) and to the spiritual realm. The controlling of nature was, after all, the perceived role of both culture and the Spirit. Thus men could legitimately dominate, regulate, and subdue women, who were considered less able to control their natural functions.

Societies of the past that embraced such an understanding of women were also hostile to men who assumed the "passive" role of females when engaging in sexual activity with other men. Historically, in many cultures of the Middle East, it is not men who penetrate other men who are viewed with derision and condemnation, but rather those who allow themselves to be penetrated. This is because such men were perceived to be assuming a role understood socially as subordinate, that is, the role of the female, the slave, and the nonadult male. That an adult male might seek and experience pleasure in such a "subordinate" sexual role has often been viewed as "inexplicable, and [. . .] attributed to pathology" (Rowson, 1991). With its roots in the patriarchal culture of the Middle East, Christianity continues to reflect understandings of gender and sexuality that are limited and constricting for many people.

- Misunderstanding and suspicion of sexuality has meant that celibacy has often been viewed by the Church as the "holiest" way of expressing one's sexual self. Even within marriage, sex was often tolerated rather than celebrated by the Church—primarily because of the Church's difficulty in recognizing and acknowledging the potential connection between sexuality and the sacred. Thus marriage itself, though recognized as a ritual, wasn't declared a "sacrament" by the Church until the Middle Ages.
- In its broadest sense a sacrament is understood within the Christian tradition as something that provides us with an experience of connection with the transforming and loving presence of God. Thus the simple experience of gardening or washing the dishes can potentially be a sacramental experience if it connects us with God; if it facilitates, in other words, an awareness of God's presence and action in our lives.
- The question thus has to be asked: Is sex only sacramental, or in other words, an experience of the transforming love of God, when it is within the parameters of heterosexual marriage and when it is open to procreation? The Church says yes, as it believes that the procreative

and unitive aspects of sex cannot be separated. Why then does the Church sanction and bless the union of couples who are past the age of procreation? Or bless marriages where one or both of the individuals involved are sterile or physically unable to procreate due to a medical condition or injury? These are important critical questions that many Catholics—in their efforts to be true to their informed consciences—feel compelled to ask. Such questions do not challenge the Church's teaching authority, but the sources and experiences that inform such authority. If these sources are flawed and if these experiences are limited, then they and the teachings that they have shaped, must be critically reexamined and reevaluated.

- Safe Staff need to be at least aware of such questions, even if they themselves are unable or unwilling to articulate them. They must also be aware of the fact that increasingly, many at the grassroots level of the Church are listening to and cherishing the stories of the Church's LGBT sons and daughters. Accordingly, many Catholics have come to a point of consciousness where they recognize that the Church's refusal to be open to the potential sacramentality of human sexual experiences outside of heterosexual marriage (experiences such as committed homosexual relationships) and the Church's resistance to celebrate women as equitable representatives of Christ stem from an inability and/or unwillingness to acknowledge the flawed sources and limited experiences that have shaped current teaching on human sexuality.

- It must also be remembered that there are numerous levels of church teaching. Although the church's teaching on homosexuality is at the level of authoritative teaching, it is not considered to be at the higher level of revealed teaching; not considered, in other words, to comprise the central truths of our faith. Authoritative teaching, on the other hand, ideally presents the church's clear position on a given issue with the understanding that this is the best that can be offered for now. Most papal encyclicals and the various declarations of councils and synods are at this level.

- Finally, the issue of conscience needs to be addressed. Fr. Joseph Ratzinger (now Pope Benedict XVI) expressed the Church's understanding of the primacy of conscience when serving as Chair of Dogmatic Theology at the University of Tübingen in 1968.

"Above the pope as an expression of the binding claim of church authority," he wrote, "stands one's own conscience, which has to be obeyed first of all, if need be against the demands of church authority" (Herbert, 1969).

In our work as Catholic educators we may well be challenged by people uncomfortable and threatened by our efforts to create environments of respect, acceptance, and safety for our LGBT students. Some critics are quick to share the view that a properly informed conscience can never contradict Church teaching. Of course, such a view sees only the magisterium, the official teaching office of the institutional Church, as the source of this informing. For many Catholics, this is highly problematic and leads to the critical question: what is the hallmark of our living faith as Catholic Christians? Is it unquestioning obedience to the Pope and the magisterium and accordingly an equating of God with the "Church as institution"? Or is it trusting openness and response to the presence and action of God within the "Church as People of God" and thus the vast and diverse arena of human life and relationships?

21. Facilitator notes that in Session 4 "The LGBT Reality and the Catholic Church," a selection of recent church teaching regarding homosexual orientation and behavior will be presented and discussed in light of the above insights regarding the history and ongoing development of church teachings.

22. Facilitator notes that there are practical (and pastorally sensitive) guidelines for responding to LGBT youths—guidelines that serve as valuable strategies in the event of a LGBT youth sharing information about awareness and/or concerns about his/her sexual identity, or of a student simply asking questions about sexual identity in general. These guidelines acknowledge the "high risk factors" associated with LGBT youths and reflect the "pastoral mandate" expressed in

much of the Church's teaching regarding sexual orientation. They will be explored further during Session 3: Coming Out.

23. Facilitator distributes Session 2 Reading Assignment to participants and asks that for the next session they read and reflect upon the anecdotal pieces that comprise this assignment.

24. Session 1 is closed with the sharing of the last two verses of the opening reflection, "Does It Matter?" (see Appendix 1).

HANDOUTS

Handout 1.1. A Teacher Reflects on the Crisis in Catholic Schools

I believe that there is a crisis among lesbian, gay, bisexual, transgender, and questioning (LGBT) youths in Catholic schools today.

This crisis is not the result of being LGBT, but rather of hearing only moral instruction on homosexuality with little to no pastoral response. The teachings of the Church on homosexuality have greatly contributed to this crisis in LGBT youths' spirituality and experience of alienation.

A first step in remedying this situation is to remember that throughout the Judeo-Christian tradition, a fundamental characteristic of the believing community was its regard for, sensitivity to, and care of its widows, aliens, and orphans, that is, the marginalized.

Students experience alienation and abandonment on a daily basis as a result of their actual or perceived sexual orientation. The manner in which a teacher can compassionately listen and support these and indeed *all* other students will either be a reflection of our Catholic faith's ancient call for solidarity with the marginalized, or an outright rejection of this call. Put another way, what's being tested by this crisis is our ability to reconcile diversity in the Body of Christ.

It is a crisis, therefore, that provides each one of us—as both Catholic educators and members of the Body of Christ—with the opportunity to build and maintain respectful, supportive, and safe schools for all students. Such courageous action is more than meeting the needs of the times. It is a way of embodying the timeless mandate of the Gospel of Jesus.

Handout 1.2. A Reflection on Human Sexuality

When a human is viewed only on the grounds of his or her sexual orientation it diminishes that person. I know this claim is stating the obvious and is found within Roman Catholic Church teaching. However, allow me to show how this principle can and has been selectively applied in views relating to heterosexual and homosexual persons.

The heterosexuality of almost all human beings is so deeply woven into the fabric of our consciousness that it has become practically invisible. That is to say, we can look upon that person as a person whereby her or his genital/sexual activity/expression does not surface in an immediate association (if it comes to mind at all). Thus my neighbor is my neighbor, my teacher is my teacher, and my boss is my boss—each heterosexual and each with a depth of personhood that exceeds the power of words. While the genital/sexual activity of these persons is sacred, it also plays a small part in the totality of their life. Moreover, even if any one of these individuals does not engage in genital/sexual acts, they can be and remain heterosexual.

However, such a balanced, just, and healthy view of people who are heterosexual is not consistently applied to the person who is homosexual. By contrast, the knowledge that someone is homosexual can conjure up images (for some at least) of specific genital/sexual activity. Thus what is missing in these associations is any appreciation for the common daily experiences of work and worship—at home or in the community—and all of the other dimensions of living that both people who are homosexual and people who are heterosexual share.

This diminished, narrow, but likely vivid construction of homosexual people in the minds of heterosexual people is neither fair nor respectful. It also does not address the underlying element of fear. This particular view of the person who is homosexual denies his or her humanity and his or her contribution as a human being, and assumes that having homosexual orientation means homosexual genital/sexual behavior.

It's as if heterosexuality is rightfully considered a noun, but homosexuality is always a verb.

Handout 1.3. Some Common Fallacies and Stereotypes of LGBT Persons

- LGBT persons represent a negligible number of people.
- LGBT persons choose to be who they are, so they deserve whatever happens to them, including discrimination and AIDS.
- Most child molesters are LGBT persons.
- You can always tell a LGBT person by how he or she looks, dresses or acts.
- Homosexuality is a type of mental illness that can be cured by appropriate psychotherapy.
- LGBT persons' lifestyles are contrary to family values as LGBT people are obsessed with sex and lead promiscuous lives.
- Homosexuality is caused by bad parenting.
- Homosexuality is caused by negative experiences with the opposite sex. All a homosexual person needs is to have some positive experiences with a member of the opposite sex.
- There are no "bisexuals." Most people are either completely homosexually or completely heterosexually oriented.
- The "gay agenda" is antifamily and is trying to destroy the institution of marriage and the family.
- The "gay agenda" wants special rights and privileges already guaranteed by the Constitution.
- LGBT persons are by nature disordered and sinners. If God really loved them, He would never have allowed them to have such an affliction.
- The Bible condemns homosexuality.
- Most LGBT persons act like pagans and show hatred toward God and organized religion.

(*Note:* Refer to information in Appendix 2—Countering Common Fallacies and Stereotypes of LGBT persons in response to specific questions/concerns about any of the above.)

Handout 1.4. Human Sexuality Definitions

Language is dynamic. It grows, changes, and develops. This is particularly true with the language of diversity and the terms ("labels") we use to identify ourselves. We must strive to be sure that our language does not demean, exclude, or offend. We must allow others to self-identify, as definitions of terms will vary for everyone. The following definitions are given to provide a starting point for discussion and understanding.

Definitions

androgynous: Usually applied to a person whose gender identity is not apparent.

biological sex or gender: Being male or female, as determined by chromosomes and body chemistry.

bisexual: A person who seeks and/or experiences physical, emotional and/or spiritual intimacy with either a man or a woman.

coming out/out of the closet/being out: Terms denoting that one is declaring or has declared openly that one is bisexual, gay, lesbian, or transgender. In contrast, to "stay in the closet" is to hide or deny one's gender identity or sexual orientation either from oneself or from others.

cross-dresser: One who, regardless of the motivation, wears the clothes, makeup, etc., assigned by society to the opposite sex. Generally, these persons do not alter their bodies. The term "crossdresser" is generally preferred over the more clinical "transvestite."

erotophobia: The fear of sexual desire.

female: One of the two biological genders. The term is generally designated based on the primary sex characteristic of having a vagina.

feminine: The gender role assigned to females.

gay: A term that some consider generic, in that it is used to describe both men and women who are attracted to the same sex. Some object to the use of the term "gay" when referring to lesbians.

gay man: A man who seeks and/or experiences physical, emotional and/or spiritual intimacy with another man.

gender: One's identification as either male or female; expressed in terms of masculinity and femininity. Gender is both biologically and culturally shaped and determined.

gender identity: An individual's basic self-conviction of being male or female. This conviction is not contingent upon the individual's biological gender/sex. The exact process by which boys and girls come to see themselves as male or female is not known. However, research indicates that gender identity develops some time between birth and three years of age (*see also* TRANSGENDER).

gender role: To interact with society as a member of a specific gender (i.e., as a man or woman) by following often arbitrary rules assigned by society that define what clothing, behaviors, thoughts, feelings, relationships, etc., are considered appropriate and inappropriate for members of each sex. What things are considered masculine, feminine, or gender neutral vary according to locations, class, occasion, time in history, and numerous other factors.

heterosexism: The system of oppression that reinforces the belief in the inherent superiority of heterosexuality and heterosexual relationships, thereby negating the lives and relationships of LGBT persons.

heterosexual: A person who experiences the fulfillment of the human need for deep connection with persons of the opposite gender. Also referred to as "straight." The expression and fulfillment of this "deep connection" may take many forms, including sexual intimacy.

heterosexual privilege: The basic civil rights and social privileges that a heterosexual person automatically receives, and which are systematically denied to LGBT persons simply because of their sexual orientation. The societal assumption and norm that all people are heterosexual.

homophobia: Negative feelings, attitudes, actions, or behaviors against LGBT people, or people perceived to be LGBT. It may also manifest as a person's fear of being perceived as LGBT. Consists of three separate components: sexism, xenophobia, and erotophobia.

homosexual: A term coined in 1869 by an early psychiatrist named Kertbery, who used it to describe persons who have sexual urges that render them physically and psychically incapable of "normal" sexual behavior. Since the word was originally used to describe a pathology, most bisexual, gay, and lesbian people today do not like to use this term to describe themselves. Homosexuality per se is no longer considered to be pathological by the American Psychiatric Association, the American Psychological Association, the American Medical Association, and many other professional organizations. The word "homosexual" is often used as a clinical descriptor when discussing discrete sexual behaviors (e.g., to describe same-sex behaviors or fantasies).

intersexed individual: People born with some combination of both male and female genitalia. Formerly known as hermaphrodites.

lesbian: A woman who seeks and/or experiences physical, emotional and/or spiritual intimacy with another woman.

LGBT: Lesbian, Gay, Bisexual, and Transgender.

male: One of the two biological genders. Normally based on the primary sex characteristic of having a penis (*see* PRIMARY SEX CHARACTERISTICS).

man: One who identifies with the masculine gender role, regardless of present sex or sexual identity.

masculine: The gender role assigned to males.

primary sex characteristics: Those primary physical characteristics that society relies on to separate the sexes—the penis for males, the vagina for females (*see* FEMALE, MALE).

queer: A term increasingly used by people who are not heterosexual in order to define themselves. Though once used as a derogatory term for LGBT persons, many LGBT people are now consciously using it as a way of reclaiming their uniqueness and power as outsiders.

sex: (1) An act, or series of acts, that humans do so as to express their sexual nature and their sexual desire, love, and affection for another. (2) The identification of biological gender.

sexism: Prejudice or discrimination based on sex, especially discrimination against women. Also, behavior, conditions, or attitudes that foster stereotypes of social roles based on biological gender.

sexual orientation: The quality within human beings that leads them to be emotionally and physically attracted to persons of one gender or the other or both. One's sexual orientation may be heterosexual (attracted to the opposite gender), homosexual (attracted to the same gender), bisexual (attracted to both genders), or asexual.

sexual reassignment surgery (SRS): A surgical procedure designed to modify one's primary sexual characteristics (genitalia) from those of one gender to those of another (penis to vagina or vagina to penis). May also include secondary surgery such as breast implants.

Symbols of Pride for the LGBT Community

Annual Gay Pride Celebration: Gay Pride celebrations or festivals are held across the United States in late June. This time was chosen in recognition of the Stonewall Inn Uprising—a three-day demonstration in New York City that began on June 27, 1969, an event often cited as spearheading the modern gay liberation movement.

 Gay Pride celebrations have three main aims: (1) to educate people about the diversity, issues, and goals of LGBT people; (2) to provide a forum for celebration of the history and accomplishments of LGBT individuals; and (3) to provide an opportunity for networking and outreach by the many businesses, services, and community organizations that welcome, serve, and/or are owned/run by LGBT people, their families, and friends.

black triangle: Lesbians and prostitutes in the Nazi work camps and death camps were forced to wear the symbol of the black triangle on their uniforms. The black triangle is now worn to honor the women previously persecuted and, as with the pink triangle, as a reclaimed symbol of resistance and pride in the face of persecution and oppression.

lambda sign: The eleventh letter in the Greek alphabet, lambda, has long been a universal gay icon.

pink triangle: The symbol of the pink triangle dates back to World War II. In 1935—four years prior to the outbreak of the war—the Nazi regime in Germany passed antihomosexual laws. Such laws stemmed from the fascist political agenda—one marked by selective populism, contempt for the weak, fear of difference, and a cult of tradition—actively promoted by Adolf Hitler, the head of the Nazi Party and the leader of Germany from 1933 to 1945.

 During the war years (1939-1945) the Nazis constructed numerous death camps wherein Jews, homosexuals, Roma, Poles, the mentally and physically handicapped, immigrants, political dissidents, and others were systematically murdered. Each of the groups targeted by the Nazi regime was identified with a symbol. For example, Jews were forced to wear a yellow Star of

David on their coats and camp uniforms, homosexuals were forced to wear pink triangles. When the camps were liberated by the Allied Powers in 1945, homosexual prisoners were the last of the various groups to be freed. In some cases, they were held for months by Allied soldiers in the same pitiful conditions that they were held by their Nazi captors.

Since 1977, the pink triangle has been adopted by the LGBT community as a symbol of the fight against oppression and the work for acceptance and inclusion. Today, the pink triangle is worn by LGBT people as a reminder of the dangers of fascism and as a symbol of resistance and pride in the face of persecution and oppression.

rainbow flag: The Rainbow Flag was designed by San Francisco artist and former military officer, Gilbert Baker. Inspired by the five-striped "Flag of the Races" (red, black, brown, yellow and white), the Rainbow Flag represents the unified diversity of the LGBT community. Baker created the original eight-colored Rainbow Flag in response to the 1978 assassination of Harvey Milk, San Francisco's first openly gay City Supervisor.

The six-striped Rainbow Flag, comprising red, orange, yellow, green, blue and purple, was introduced in 1979 by the Paramount Flag Company. In 1985 it was accepted by the International Association of Lesbian and Gay Pride as an internationally-recognized LGBT symbol of Pride.

trans: An umbrella term covering people of the transgender community.

transgender: A term used to include transsexuals, transvestites, and cross-dressers. It can also represent a person who, like a transsexual, transitions—sometimes with the help of hormone therapy and/or cosmetic surgery—to live in the gender role of choice, but has not undergone sexual reassignment surgery (SRS). Sexual orientation among transgender people varies from individual to individual.

transgender symbol: Created by linking the two internationally accepted symbols for male and female within a circle, the transgender symbol represents everyone, excluding no one. Some have suggested that the transgender's destiny is to restore the connection between man and woman. The circle is a universal symbol of wholeness, and represents the wholeness of a society that includes the transgender individual. The misdirection of a society that ridicules and excludes transgender people is implied.

transsexual: A person whose gender identity is opposite to his or her biological gender. Such individuals feel a consistent and overwhelming desire to "transition," that is, live their lives as members of the opposite gender. Most, although not all, transsexuals actively desire and complete sexual reassignment surgery (SRS). However, regardless of whether a transsexual person has undergone SRS, the transsexual community prefers that the pronouns (e.g., he/she, his/hers) referring to gender identity—rather than to biological gender—be used when referring to them.

transvestite: The clinical name for a *cross-dresser*—a person who dresses in the clothing of the opposite gender. Generally, these individuals do not desire or pursue any kind of sexual reassignment surgery. Sexual orientation varies from individual to individual.

woman: One who identifies with the feminine gender role, regardless of present gender or gender identity.

xenophobia: Fear and hatred of strangers and foreigners or of anything that is strange or foreign.

Handout 1.5. LGBT Youths: Some Basic Pastoral Assumptions

1. All student, staff, and family deserve a safe, supportive school environment that fosters positive self-esteem, respect for others, and academic success.
2. Youths need to feel safe and secure in order to learn and to grow.
3. As a highly stigmatized and invisible minority, LGBT issues are very complex and require a special degree of sensitivity.
4. We are called by the Gospel of our brother Jesus and committed in conscience to work for:
   - Fostering school environments that truly value human diversity.
   - Reducing high-risk behavior among LGBT youths.*
   - Eliminating harassment and violence against LGBT students, staff, and families.

(* High-risk behavior among LGBT youths is examined in detail in Session 3 "Coming Out.")

Handout 1.6. Recent Research Findings Concerning LGBT Youths in Catholic Schools*

LGBT Students in Catholic Schools

In the 2001 and 2003 surveys combined, 3.5 percent of the students (N = 63) attended Catholic schools. This percentage is similar to the national percentage of secondary students nationwide attending Catholic schools (approximately 4.3 percent).**

Biased Language

As shown in Figure 1.1, the vast majority of Catholic school students heard homophobic remarks frequently or often. The incidence of homophobic remarks was similar between Catholic school students and all others. In contrast, students in Catholic schools reported sexist and racist remarks in school less often than students in all other types of schools.

There were no differences between Catholic school students and other students in terms of the frequency of faculty or staff intervention regarding homophobic, racist, or sexist remarks. However, as shown in Figure 1.2, students for all types of schools reported that faculty or staff intervened much less often with homophobic remarks than with other types of remarks.

School Safety

- Seventy-three percent of Catholic school students reported feeling unsafe in school because of their sexual orientation and 46 percent reported feeling unsafe because of their gender expression.
- Twenty-seven percent of Catholic school students reported missing at least one class and 22 percent reported missing at least one entire day of school because of feeling unsafe.
- Eighty-one percent of Catholic school students reported being verbally harassed in school because of their sexual orientation and 65.1 percent because of their gender expression.

School Supports

Catholic school students were just as likely to report having a teacher who was supportive of LGBT students as students in all other types of schools (90.6 percent and 89.6 percent, respectively). Catholic school students, however, were less likely to report having openly LGBT faculty/staff or other openly LGBT students.

As shown in Figure 1.3, although Catholic school students were not significantly different from other types of students in being comfortable in raising LGBT issues with their teachers, school counselors, and school nurses, they were much less likely to report being comfortable raising these issues with their principals and in their classes.

---

*GLSEN (2004). *Catholic School Facts from GLSEN's National School Climate Surveys*. New York: Author. Kosciw, J.G. (2004). *The 2003 National School Climate Survey: The School-related Experiences of Our Nation's Gay, Bisexual, and Transgender Youths*. New York: GLSEN, Reprinted with permission.

**According to the National Center for Education Statistics, there were 14.2 million students enrolled in secondary schools in 1999, approximately 600,000 in Catholic secondary schools.

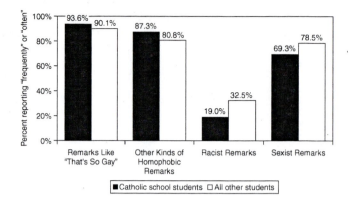

FIGURE 1.1. Biased Language in School: Catholic School Students versus All Others

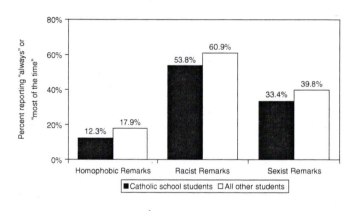

FIGURE 1.2. Teacher Intervention Re: Biased Language: Catholic School Students versus All Others

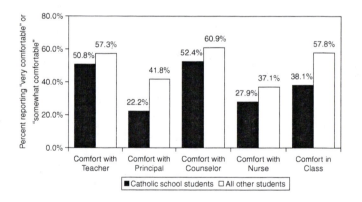

FIGURE 1.3. Comfort Discusing LGBT Issues in School: Catholic School Students versus All Others

Source: GLSEN (2004). *Catholic School Facts from GLSEN's National School Climate Surveys.* New York: Author. Kosciw, J.G. (2004). *The 2003 National School Climate Survey: The School-related Experiences of Our Nation's Gay, Bisexual, and Transgender Youths.* New York: GLSEN. Reprinted with permission.

Handout 1.7. Important Points Concerning Psychosocial Aspects of LGBT Youths

1. LGBT teens will grow into LGBT adults; what happens in their teen years will very often determine the quality and outcome of their adult lives.
2. Can a school be considered as fully committed to diversity when it does not address the needs of LGBT students and their families?
3. As in the case of other minorities, a school environment that respects the diversity of LGBT students must be intentionally created—it does not just happen.
4. Homophobia is a spiritual, as well as psychosocial affliction. Addressing homophobia helps the whole school community, by:
   - Reducing sexual acting out and other negative behaviors.
   - Broadening gender roles so that more aspirations and dreams can be realized.
   - Making same-sex friendships a safer source of support and nurturance for all students.
   - Helping to build the Body of Christ.

Handout 1.8. A Selection of Kinsey's Findings

- Thirty-seven percent of the total male population has at least some overt homosexual experience to the point of orgasm between adolescence and old age. This accounts for nearly two males out of every five that one may meet.
- Ten percent of males are more or less exclusively homosexual for at least three years between the ages of sixteen and fifty-five. This is one male in ten in the white population.
- Eight percent of males are exclusively homosexual for at least three years between the ages of sixteen and fifty-five. This is one male in every thirteen.
- Four percent of white males are exclusively homosexual throughout their lives, after the onset of adolescence.
- The findings on homosexual behaviors of females are slightly lower but equally insightful.

Kinsey was convinced that,

> If all persons with any trace of homosexual history, or those who were predominantly homosexual, were eliminated from the population today, there is no reason for believing that the incidence of the homosexual in the next generation would be materially reduced. The homosexual has been a significant part of human sexual activity since the dawn of history, primarily because it is an expression of capacities that are basic in the human animal. (Kinsey et al., 1948: 666)

Interestingly, Kinsey felt that the high incidence of homosexual experience among high school age males was of particular importance:

> These are the males who most often condemn the homosexual, most often ridicule and express disgust for such activity, and most often punish other males for their homosexuality. And yet, this is the group which has the largest amount of homosexual activity. . . . As a group, these males may strenuously deny that their sexual contacts have anything to do with homosexuality; but the full and complete record indicates that many of them have stronger psychic reactions to other males than they admit. (Kinsey et al., 1948: 384)

Handout 1.9. Sexual Identity: An Application of Theological Anthropology

Debate continues about whether or not homosexuality is an orientation or a "preference" that involves personal choice. An approach to the pastoral care of youths assumes that sexual identity (inclusive of orientation) is not a "preference" but a basic orientation toward relationship.

Orientation toward relationship is an essential element of being human, of being made in the image of God. It is actually one's *esse,* one's way of being in the world. Being orientated toward others is one's fundamental spiritual legacy.

Such an understanding is supported by two key points from theological anthropology:

1. *Human beings are fundamentally oriented toward God*

An extraordinary legacy of concepts and language from theological anthropology can be applied to a pastoral approach to students facing questions about sexual identity. As early as Aristotle, human beings are described as being oriented toward a purpose or end. This viewpoint later influenced St. Augustine, as can be observed in one of his most quoted passages from his *Confessions:*

> . . . *quia fecisti nos ad te et inquietum est cor nostrum, donec requiescat in te, da mihi domine* . . . The thought of You [God] stirs [humans] so deeply they cannot be content unless [they] praise You, because You have made [them] for Yourself and [their] hearts find no peace until [they] rest in You. (Augustine of Hippo, 2001)

Although for Aristotle, one's ultimate end was happiness, he declares that human beings will not be content until they find their end in God. Augustine writes, "You have made us for Yourself." The Latin, *ad* translated as "for" is a common translation. Yet *ad* literally translates, "to be toward," in basic direction and purpose. Thus a closer reading of the Latin would translate, "You have made us to be towards Yourself, O God." Therefore, being human means being created to be toward God as one's ultimate fulfillment.

Building upon both Aristotle and Augustine, Saint Thomas Aquinas even describes heaven itself as a state of being in the presence of God—who is the culmination of earthly hungers and yearnings. Further, Aquinas emphasizes that the human being is both soul and body oriented toward God by necessity, not by the choice of the will. In other words, to seek the supreme good and happiness is inherent in all people.

The following question can be raised: how can humans be free if they were made to be toward God by nature? To answer this question, Thomas, in *Summa Theologica 1, 82-83,* explains the difference between *voluntas* and *liberum arbitrium—literally, the fundamental difference between will and choice.*

That human beings seek the final good is part of their very nature and not left to personal choice. At the same time, human beings are free to choose the means to happiness, *liberum arbitrium.* The way to happiness occurs from choice. Thus human beings seek happiness by necessity, *voluntas,* and freely choose the way toward that happiness, *liberum arbitrium.*

2. *Human knowledge of an all-loving God is revealed in Jesus Christ and mediated through relationships with others and creation*

God is not the first thing human beings know. They move from knowledge of things to knowledge of God. In the finite, human beings receive glimpses of the Infinite. Augustine writes:

But what do I love when I love you? Not the beauty of body nor the gracefulness of temporal rhythm, not the brightness of light so friendly to the eyes, not the sweet and various melodies of songs, not the fragrance of flowers and ointments and spices, not manna and honey; not limbs receptive to fleshly embraces: I love not these when I love my God. And yet I do love a kind of light, the melody, the fragrance, the food, the embrace of my inner self: Where that light shines into my soul which no place can contain, and where that voice sounds which time does not take away, and where that fragrance smells which no wind scatters, and where there is that flavor which eating does not diminish, and where there is that clinging that no satiety will separate. This is what I love when I love my God. (Augustine of Hippo, 2001, Book X.6)

Thus God is not the first thing humans "know"—they move from knowledge of things material to knowledge of the immaterial God. God is revealed in the person of Jesus Christ, and continues to be mediated (expressed and reflected) through human relationships. Accordingly, the capacity to conceive of the unconditional, omnipotent love of God is profoundly influenced by our experiences of love on earth: parental, peer, spousal, and professional relationships, and so on.

Therefore, it is crucial to offer pastoral care to youths with questions concerning sexual identity because these questions impact their daily interaction with others and ultimately their capacity to conceive of and experience the transforming love of God.

Handout 1.10. Sexual Identity: A Composite of Four Continuums

Sexual identity consists of four continuums that address four aspects of identity. Figure 1.4 illustrates sexual identity as a composition of biological sex, gender identity, gender expression, and sexual orientation.

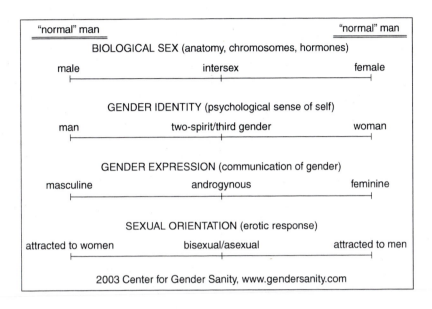

FIGURE 1.4. Diagram of Sex and Gender (*Source:* Janis Walworth, *Diagram of Sex and Gender,* Center for Gender Sanity, 1998, revised 2003. Reprinted with permission.)

Handout 1.11. A Reflection on the Ongoing Development of Church Doctrine

The Catholic Church has rightly denounced biblical fundamentalism. It has yet to denounce, however, doctrinal fundamentalism. All forms of fundamentalism are ultimately idolatrous.

Church doctrines, like scripture, should serve to point beyond themselves to God. They should not be taken as God. Equating doctrine with God is dangerous. It lends itself to dehumanizing situations by failing to acknowledge the role that human experience has and continues to play in the development of our understanding of God, and our articulation of this understanding through our theological and doctrinal statements.

What is the relationship between experience and doctrine? The relationship can be best demonstrated by the following quote by author Mary Pellauer: "If there is anything worth calling theology, it is listening to people's stories; listening to them and cherishing them" (quoted in Norris, 2001).

The sentiment expressed in these words reflects the reality that the pastoral concerns of today, the real-life experiences of contemporary people, comprise the raw material for tomorrow's theological statements and church doctrines. This pattern is nothing new. Human experience has always been the fertile ground for divine revelation. When this experience of the sacred by individuals and communities is prayerfully and reverently reflected upon and listened to, it has the potential to shape the theological development of the Church, the People of God.

This fact in no way reduces the importance of the theological and ecclesiastical teachings we have today. Rather, this pattern of development, this ongoing process of which we are all a part, should remind us that the teachings we have in place today are the product of how past generations, with all their gifts and limitations, viewed and responded to the presence of the sacred discerned in all aspects of human life—including human sexuality.

LGBT Catholics and their families who know and declare that their lives and relationships are a gift from God are accused by some of wanting to "change the church." Fueling this accusation is the erroneous belief that the Catholic Church is somehow unchanged and unchangeable, somehow incapable of growing and developing. Yet if this were the case then not only would the Catholic Church still be teaching that the sun revolves around the earth, it would also be ambiguous on the moral issue of slavery and hostile to the idea of democracy.

A static understanding of Church stems in part from a model of revelation that sees truths handed down from on high—complete and unchangeable. Yet as Pope John XXIII reminded us, "We are not on earth to guard a museum but to cultivate a flowering garden of life." Such a statement implies that revelation filters upward through human life and experience, and that revelation is ongoing. It's a concept that's both wondrous and unsettling—and for fundamentalists, one that is extremely threatening. Embracing the reality on unfolding revelation propels us out of our comfortable ghettos of formulated answers and into compassionate—at times challenging—engagement with the world. And it is through such engagement that we are called to discern and incarnate—personally and communally—the Reign of God in every aspect of life.

Catholics open to the development of Church teaching have also been accused of basing their morality on cultural trends. Such suspicion of culture denies the reality that it is through a range of relational contexts that the Church, as the People of God, has always experienced God's transforming presence. For example, in the past women were judged to be incapable of many of the things men could do. That view has been nearly erased due to the dramatic emergence and involvement of women in Church and society.

Those of us—gay and straight—within the Catholic Church who embrace a theology of sexuality that is reality based and scientifically supported, understand our efforts as revealing God's love in the lives and relationships of all people—gay, lesbian, bisexual, and transgender people included. We're doing what our brother Jesus did—making visible the Reign of God already in our midst but so often hidden by oppressive structures and by ignorance and fear.

History shows that the overcoming of such fear and ignorance takes time. Nevertheless, a growing number of Catholics look forward to the day when the Church's teaching on sexuality joyously proclaims God's presence in the lives and relationships of LGBT people.

READING ASSIGNMENT

(To be distributed at the end of Session 1)

Moving Beyond Fear

Young LGBT Catholics share their experiences and insights for creating safe schools and parishes.

On October 11, 2000, the Catholic Pastoral Committee on Sexual Minorities (CPCSM) launched its Fall Outreach Luncheon Series with a presentation and discussion led by three young lesbian, gay, bisexual, transgendered (LGBT) Catholics.

The "youths panel" focused on the role and work of parish youths ministries and the various ways that LGBT-related issues are addressed at the parish level and in both Catholic and non-Catholic high schools.

Three young Catholics—Rachel, a public high school student; Brendan, a Catholic high school alum; and Tony, a parish youth minister—thoughtfully and articulately shared their experiences and insights with an attentive audience comprised primarily of Catholic pastoral and youths ministers.

Brendan's opening comment set a somber tone for the event as he grimly noted that his life as a gay youth at a Catholic high school was "really not a good experience." He said that in both the school and the parish community "whenever any LGBT issue came up, which was very rare, it was always very quickly shut down or framed within the context of 'this is something the Pope condemns,' or 'this is something we can't talk about right now.'"

Brendan also experienced direct harassment by fellow students. His teachers were dismissive of his plight and informed him that he would "just have to deal with it." With his parents' support, Brendan soon transferred to a new, non-Catholic high school.

Reflecting upon his experience of Catholic education, Brendan was adamant that there has to be an acknowledgment of the degree of harassment experienced by LGBT youths, and that this problem is just as valid and in need of attention as the problem of racism. "I would have benefited from an anonymous support group at the school. I would have attended such a group," he said.

Brendan also recommended that a LGBT perspective be integrated into the Catholic educational system. "We need to work at helping schools develop a more rounded curriculum," he said. "We need to encourage teachers to cover or at least acknowledge a LGBT perspective." He recalled that throughout his education, the only reference to LGBT people that he had heard was in relation to AIDS: "I thought the only people who were gay were dying of AIDS."

BRENDAN: Issues like sexual orientation need to be covered not just from a narrow Roman Catholic view, but from one that is truly educative and is prepared to look at all sides of an issue. . . .
If I had been taught in an objective way, if I had had access to basic information and been treated fairly as the other students, my experience of Catholic education would have probably been very different.

Rachel, the panel's second speaker, is currently a student at a Twin Cities public high school. She offered an alternative to Brendan's experience of "coming out" in the high school setting: "I had a wonderful experience," she declared, "and I hope to present it as an ideal model."

At Rachel's high school there are currently forty students who are part of a LGBT support group. There's also a Gay/Straight Alliance (GSA), and staff members who are recognized throughout the school community as "safe staff," that is, as staff members to whom students, struggling with questions about sexuality and sexual identity, can turn. Rachel suggested that one very basic way of cultivating a safe and supportive atmosphere for LGBT students is by preventing hate speech. "At my school, when the word 'gay' is used as an insult, a teacher steps up and says that this is not okay. The teachers at my school have a tremendous influence on [us] and what [our] tolerance level will be."

Proactive visibility is also a key factor in establishing a welcoming environment for LGBT youths, according to Rachel. "Rainbow stickers, posters explaining to our students that we welcome diversity, that we're accepting—people who are questioning take all of this in."

The GSA provided by Rachel's high school played an important role in her positive coming out experience.

RACHEL: It helped me come out not only to my friends, but to my parents and family. It helped eliminate a lot of the fear. . . . There's a lot of pressure and anxiety associated with coming out. At my previous school it was stressed that coming out was a flaw, that one was not a good person if you were gay. At my new school I was able to move beyond the fear.

Tony's contribution to the discussion came from the perspective of a parish-based youth minister. He notes that for every event organized and publicized by his parish, there is a line that reads, "All are welcome." LGBT issues, however, are still not talked about in the parish setting—they are a "non-subject."

Tony believes that this is a problem typical of suburban parishes. He notes that the hardest aspect of his work as a parish-based youth minister is building a youth program that openly acknowledges and welcomes "gay *and* straight" youths. To date, he has been unable to include such a welcome on any official invitation or announcement. To do so "would cause too much of a ruckus, yet it's something that needs to happen, but it takes time."

In relation to catechesis, Tony encourages everyone to look for ways to talk about homosexuality in topics outside of morality.

TONY: It seems that the only time we hear about homosexuality [is] when we're talking about sexual morality . . . yet Church teachings cover much more—social justice, non-violence, compassion. So let's talk about homosexuality when we're talking about justice, compassion, community.

CPCSM member Mary Lynn Murphy, who moderated the discussion, noted that teachers, youth ministers, and others interacting with young people must remember that many youths are uncertain about the spectrum of sexual orientation and don't necessarily know whether they're gay or straight.

MARY: It's a confusing time. My perspective, as the mother of a young gay man, is that rather than encourage our kids to label themselves, encourage them simply to be open to their questions and to value diversity in all its forms.

Mary, speaking for CPCSM, also posed the following critical question: "Does the doctrinal position of the official Church discourage LGBT youths from seeking pastoral help and support?"

CPCSM believes that the "official" position is extremely negative and, in the long term, hopeless for LGBT youths. In CPCSM's Safe Schools Initiative, teachers are reminded that all teenagers are called to celibacy at this particular stage of their lives. Yet very deliberately, CPCSM does not endorse the "official" Church's view that LGBT teens are called to lifelong celibacy.

(*Note:* Session 4 "The LGBT Reality and the Catholic Church" will explore this issue in greater depth.)

It is for this reason that the ministry of CPCSM comes under fire from others within the Church who, for whatever reason, fail to hear and respond to Christ's message of inclusiveness and liberation mediated through the experiences and insights of LGBT people.

CPCSM's "youth panel" demonstrated that indeed the Spirit is powerfully speaking through such individuals and in the process, calling the entire Church to conversion and renewal. CPCSM welcomes such a call and will continue in its Spirit-inspired work with and for LGBT Catholics and thus for wider Church reform and renewal. We welcome all—gay and straight—to join us in this challenging yet rewarding work.

After reading "Moving Beyond Fear," reflect upon and respond to the following questions:

1. How are LGBT-related issues addressed within your parish? How are they addressed within your Catholic high school and other high schools with which you are familiar?

2. Why do you think any talk about LGBT-related issues was "always very quickly shut down" in Brendan's Catholic high school? How else was it sometimes dealt with? How useful are such responses? Can you think of any other ways to respond?

3. Brendan maintains that he would have benefited from an "anonymous support group" at his school. How feasible would such a group be in your school? What would be some barriers preventing the establishing of such a group? Where might support come from for the establishment of such a group? How about a gay/straight alliance as a more comfortable starting point for your school?

4. Brendan recommends a "more rounded curriculum," one that acknowledges an LGBT perspective. How might such a curriculum look? What might it entail? Could you see your school's curriculum acknowledging the achievements and/or perspectives of LGBT people? Why/why not? What other related resources might be used to enhance such a curriculum?

5. Brendan notes that "issues like sexual orientation need to be covered not just from a narrow [Roman] Catholic view but from one that is truly educative and is prepared to look at all sides of an issue." What does this mean to you? What would be some examples of looking at all sides of an issue? How does your school understand "Catholic education"? Can Catholic education be objective?

6. How would you respond if you heard a student call another student "gay," "fag," or "dyke"? How would you respond if you heard a student using a racial epithet? Would, or should, your manner of response differ in either case? Why/why not?

7. What were the ways in which Rachel's school environment ensured a positive "coming out"? Which of these ways, or others that you can think of, would be possible in your school? How would you go about implementing them?

8. Like Brendan, Tony too calls for a broader way of talking about homosexuality. Can you envision talking about homosexuality when you are speaking in class about justice, compassion, or community? Try and think of an example to share with the group at the beginning of Session 2.

9. What are your thoughts on Mary Lynn's perspective as the mother of a gay young man? How do you see it similar to the perspective of the mother of a straight young man? How might it be different?

First Steps

A teacher recalls the launching of safe staff training at her Catholic high school:

I hope I get at least five teachers . . . oh please . . . at least five!

This was the hope that ran through my mind when I first asked our faculty and staff whether they would be willing to be trained as "safe staff." Such a staff person, I had noted, is an adult who has received specialized training in the psychosocial and theological/spiritual aspects of LGBT youths and, as a result, has made a specific commitment to deal with LGBT youths in a pastorally sensitive and nonjudgmental manner.

This is a fancy way of saying that a safe staff person is someone who loves and cares for all students and who especially wants our LGBT students to feel welcome, safe, and valued at their school.

So I was hoping for at least five teachers who would be willing to commit to learning more about the invisible minority in our school. What I got was five times five teachers! There were twenty-five teachers who signed up to be trained as safe staff—and I was thrilled.

We began our training in October 1997 and finished our last session in March 1998. Over the course of those months, other teachers came to me asking to be included in the training. Accordingly, we soon had a waiting list for future trainings.

What touched me most were the personal stories. One young man—a 1988 graduate of our school—told of his experience of being a gay student. He never told anyone in school about his sexual identity and recalled feeling isolated and depressed. He even turned to drugs as a way to numb his pain.

While not all LGBT students struggle with depression and chemical use, it is true that in many ways our gay and lesbian students are an invisible minority. Our hope is that by training our faculty and staff we can be open and loving to our LGBT students and walk with them on their high school journey.

Our safe staff group chose a symbol to hang in our classrooms and offices. We chose a rainbow bumper sticker with the words "Celebrate Diversity" written across the rainbow. We hang this symbol with pride.

Our prayer is that the symbol says that we will give our LGBT students a voice, a safe place to learn, a community of compassion and support that is nonjudgmental.

We pray that our symbol says we will not tolerate jokes or derogatory remarks about LGBT persons or issues, that we will not allow others to intimidate or harass students about their sexual identity, and that we will not allow anyone to cast a negative light on the human dignity that God has bestowed on every single person in our school.

After reading "First Steps," reflect upon and respond to the following questions:

1. How does the teacher who wrote this article define a safe staff person? After reading the first two articles in this reading assignment, how would you define a safe staff person? Could you expand upon this definition? How?

2. What message do the teachers in the article hope their chosen safe staff symbol will relay to students? What are your thoughts about such a message? How does/might your school— with or without a symbol—relay this message to LGBT students?

"Love Them Anyway"

A Catholic high school teacher reviews John E. Fortunato's book, Embracing the Exile.

John E. Fortunato's book, *Embracing the Exile,* is about pain and sadness. Yet I finished it with a sense of joy and peace.

Fortunato, a gay psychotherapist, has written a sensitive account of his personal journey as both a therapist and a gay Christian. He writes movingly of his growing up, his wonder at his natural spirituality, and his sense of joy in his early Catholic experiences.

This state of consciousness is short-lived, as he soon comes wrenchingly into conflict with the "real world's" response to his emerging gayness.

Fortunato chronicles his experience of coming out, his split with the Church and his family, and his encounters with discrimination. He is refreshingly objective about himself as a young man coming to terms with his homosexuality and what it meant in terms of his relationship with the rest of the world.

He reaches a point of despair about people and how they have abused him. In a dialogue with God about the cruelty and evil of others, he asks: "What do I do with them?" God's answer is to "love them anyway."

It is Fortunato's struggle with this command and his eventual understanding of it that gives the book its personal touch. I found truly fascinating his ability to describe how this conversion within himself led him to become a more effective therapist.

I also trained as a therapist and am a teacher in a Catholic high school. Although I'm straight, I felt a strong sense of empathy toward this process of understanding that life will not always be what one wants, nor will it always be fair. Perhaps my understanding comes from dealing with the pain of teenagers who, in their developmental stage, all feel that they are exiles—unwelcome and strange.

The core of Fortunato's book is his analysis of how, by separating psychotherapy (with its emphasis on ego) and spirituality (with its emphasis on letting go of the ego), we miss some valuable integration and potential for transcendence. Psychologically, we attempt to avoid our pain by control. We create frameworks, paradigms, and plans, and when we experience a situation beyond our control, we experience a "breakdown"; our elaborate systems have failed us.

Fortunato explains that in our attempt to avoid pain and anxiety we only wear ourselves out. He elaborates that gay people, because of the insolubility of many of their problems, have a valuable gift to give the rest of society. While straight people can receive support from their families as they resolve issues such as racism and sexism, gay people often find themselves more isolated. Fortunato sees this isolation as a form of exile. Although there has been progress, injustices toward gay people persist and in many instances family and friends reject them.

It is from this place of rejection and exile that gay people can develop a stronger sense of self and recognize their gifts—including the potential to model a way of living that can embrace life with all of its injustices.

Fortunato uses Elisabeth Kübler-Ross's stages of coming to terms with death as a model for how many of his clients finally come to a place of acceptance. Not only acceptance of their own gayness, but an acceptance of the injustices they may have suffered and have yet to suffer.

The therapeutic process utilizes these stages of denial, bargaining, anger, depression, and finally acceptance. Gay people ultimately have to learn to grieve that their lives will always contain a vast amount of pain and unfairness. But so do we all, in our own ways.

All of us experience some form of exile: the parent who dies too soon, the parent who was not there for us, the marriage that has failed, the accident that changes our life. All of us have irreconcilable losses. It is our acceptance of loss and our movement forward with life that makes life meaningful—even inspirational.

There is much to reflect upon in Fortunato's book. I am glad I read it. It not only gave me a deeper understanding of how gay men and lesbians feel, but it also gave me some insight into myself and my own life. Take time to read this one. You won't be sorry.

After reading "Love Them Anyway," reflect upon and respond to the following questions.

1. How do you think the writer of this article benefited most from reading John Fortunato's book, *Embracing the Exile*?

2. In reviewing Fortunato's book, the writer of this article notes that "it is from [a] place of rejection and exile that gay people can develop a stronger sense of sense of self and recognize their gifts–including the potential to model a way of living that can embrace life with all its injustices." What are your thoughts on this statement?

Session 2

Defining Safe Staff

A safe staff person is someone who loves and cares for all students and who especially wants our LGBT students to feel welcome, safe and valued at their school.

Catholic High School Teacher

Topics Explored

- Defining safe staff.
- Roles and responsibilities of safe staff.
- Attitudes toward differences: the Riddle Scale.
- Qualities of a LGBT ally.
- Understanding homophobia and heterosexism.
- Reducing homophobia and responding to harassment in the school environment.

Recommended Equipment/Resources

Easel with pad and markers
Notepads, pens, and pencils
Masking tape
Prayer: "Our Children and Students as Gifts" (see Appendix 1)

Handouts

2.1　Defining Safe Staff/The Role and Responsibilities of Safe Staff
2.2　Attitudes Toward Differences: The Riddle Scale
2.3　Qualities of a LGBT Ally
2.4　Homophobia and Heterosexism
2.5　Heterosexism: Another Pillar of the Power Structure
2.6　How Homophobia and Heterosexism Hurt Adolescents
2.7　Eleven Suggestions for Reducing Homophobia in Your Environment
2.8　Responding to Harassment: Dos and Don'ts

Creating Safe Environments for LGBT Students
© 2007 by The Haworth Press, Inc. All rights reserved.
doi:10.1300/5723_04

Format

1. Facilitator begins Session 2 by sharing the prayer written by the mother of a gay child and entitled "Our Children and Students as Gifts" (see Appendix 1).

2. Facilitator reminds participants that what brings them together for this and future sessions is a deep longing to reach out to all students in their care, and especially to those who because of issues regarding sexual identity/orientation, may feel themselves to be unreachable.

3. Participants discuss their responses to the articles contained in Session 2 Reading Assignment; in particular, some of the definitions for "safe staff" that participants came up with.

4. Facilitator notes that for some, the term "safe staff" is problematic as it implies that those who have not been officially trained are unsafe. In some schools, alternative names have been devised. One Catholic high school in Minnesota, for instance, chose the term "anchor staff" and the symbol of the anchor to represent them. The anchor was chosen as it is one of the earliest Christian symbols and represents stability. The faculty and staff in that particular school, who identify as anchor staff, see themselves as offering stability and safety to all students, and recognize that the life and teaching of Jesus—grounded in radical inclusiveness and justice—represent the ultimate anchor.

5. Participants brainstorm the role and responsibilities of safe staff and then observe and discuss Handout 2.1 "Defining Safe Staff/The Role and Responsibilities of Safe Staff." Note that the roles and responsibilities listed in Handout 2.1 are advocated by a Catholic high school teacher.

6. Participants view and discuss Dorothy Riddle's *Scale of Attitudes Toward Differences* (Handout 2.2), match their attitude toward LGBT people with one of the scale's eight levels of attitude, and if willing, share with the group where they see themselves on this scale. Note that at the very least, all educators need to be at the "support" level. This level is characterized by a commitment to actively work to safeguard the rights of those who are different. Participants discuss the position on the Riddle Scale of various components of their school community—school board, school policy, student body.

Facilitator also notes that support and affirmation of LGBT students are not the same as promotion of homosexuality—a charge often leveled at Safe School initiatives. To promote is to place an idea, or group, at a higher level than other ideas and groups. Clearly, in supporting and affirming LGBT students we are not placing them above other students. Neither are we saying that being LGBT is preferable to being heterosexual.

Another point to remember is that promoting diversity is not the same thing as promoting a specific group. A school community can and should expend energy and resources in promoting diversity, that is, respect for all. However, such efforts are not equivalent to promoting any particular group.

Finally, being uncomfortable and being prejudiced are two completely different things. Discomfort is a sensation that one cannot control, whereas prejudice is disliking a group for misinformed reasons. We need to be conscious of our reasons for disliking a certain group of people and challenge ourselves to critically reevaluate the reasons and sources for such dislike.

7. With awareness of the minimal expectation in terms of attitude toward LGBT persons, participants brainstorm some practical qualities of any individual who identifies him/herself as an ally of LGBT persons. Safe staff are one type of ally to LGBT persons. After this "brain-storming" session participants view and discuss Handout 2.3 "Qualities of an LGBT Ally." Again, note that this handout was originally prepared by a Catholic high school teacher.

8. Participants view and discuss Handout 2.4 "Homophobia and Heterosexism."

9. Facilitator shares Handout 2.5 "Heterosexism: Another Pillar of the Power Structure"—and elicits responses from participants. Facilitator emphasizes that the whole structure represents

society and how the various "isms" function to support those in power at the top while keeping "down" those who are marginalized, forcing them to experience the weight and pain of oppression.

10. Facilitator notes that any school that claims to provide a safe environment for its students will work to reduce, if not eradicate homophobia. Facilitator shares Handout 2.6 "How Homophobia and Heterosexism Hurt Adolescents" and elicits responses from participants.

11. In light of their responses to Handouts 2.4, 2.5, and 2.6, participants brainstorm ideas for addressing homophobia in the classroom and/or school environment. Participants then view and discuss Handout 2.7 "Eleven Suggestions for Reducing Homophobia in Your Environment."

12. Participants observe and discuss Handout 2.8 "Responding to Harassment: Dos and Don'ts"—comprised of guidelines proposed by a classroom teacher in a Catholic high school.

13. In light of the "Harassment Dos and Don'ts" and the "Suggestions for Reducing Homophobia," participants discuss and role-play the following scenarios in groups of four to five:

- During an afternoon class one student begins taunting another by calling him a "fag." The student being taunted gets up and runs out of the classroom. Some of the remaining students laugh while others sit in stunned silence. How do you respond? Where does your primary attention go? What do you do next?

- On entering your classroom, you walk in on a group of students speculating on the sexual orientation of each faculty member. You are known by these students to be heterosexual and they attempt to engage you in their game, coaxing you to share inputs about the private lives of other teachers. Do you let this pass as innocent tomfoolery or do you challenge these students? How do you justify your decision?

- Doing a discussion in your sociology class about the history of racial prejudice, a couple of students who have been "goofing off" during class call each other, in a seemingly innocent manner, "fag" and "homo." They say these things loud enough for all to hear. The bell will be ringing in a few minutes. Do you wait it out and let it pass or do you respond to it right then and there? How do you justify your decision?

- A male student is the only boy enrolled in a home economics class. Other male students learn about this and harass him throughout the day. They call him a "sissy-fag," a "skirt," "fairy," and "fem." They also ask him why he wants to act like a woman. This student comes to you in tears and asks you to give the necessary permission for him to drop the class. Do you let him just drop the class or do you take a different approach? If so, what approach do you take?

- A student you referred to the LGBT support group had originally declared that she was a lesbian. She now comes back to you and shares that after careful consideration, she is actually bisexual. You are also aware that other gay and lesbian students have been taunting this student and accusing her of being afraid of coming out and of hiding behind the bisexual label. These students insist there is no such thing as bisexuality. The student complains to you that it is now harder to deal with being a bisexual than it was to deal with being a lesbian. She asks your advice about how to handle all the new tension she is experiencing. How do you respond? Why?

- You are aware of a student in your class who lives with his divorced gay father. The man has full custody of his son. He also lives with both his son and his partner. The student is having a great deal of difficulty as he frequently hears derogatory comments from his classmates about his "unnatural" family, his "fag fathers," and about his classmates' belief that by remaining with them he too will become a "fag." The student becomes increasingly distraught and reveals to you his plans to run away from home. What should you do? Why?

- You are teaching a history lesson and you mention a few historical persons known to be gay, lesbian, bisexual, or transgender and the impact of their sexual orientation on their life's work and achievements. A student asks why he has to learn "this kind of fag stuff?" How do you respond? Why?

- A gay student confides in you that he spends many late nights visiting gay chat rooms on his family's computer. To his knowledge, his parents are not aware of this and he has yet to go and meet anyone he has chatted with online. He says though, that he will meet up with someone if he connects with "the right guy." Finally, he states that he prefers this way of contacting other gay men over having peer relationships outside school. How would you respond to this situation?

14. To conclude Session 2, facilitator distributes Session 3 Reading Assignment to participants and asks that for the next session they read and reflect upon the anecdotal pieces that comprise this assignment.

HANDOUTS

Handout 2.1. Defining Safe Staff

A safe staff person in a Catholic high school is an adult staff person who has received specialized training in the psychosocial and theological-spiritual aspects of the LGBT youths' experience and, as a result, has made a specific commitment to deal with LGBT youths in a pastorally sensitive and nonjudgmental manner.

The use of the rainbow symbol—or some other type of symbol, such as an anchor or lighthouse—to designate the office of a safe staff person, or any other safe school space explicitly denotes a commitment by the safe staff person to be understanding, supportive, and trustworthy if a gay, lesbian, bisexual, or transgender youths—or any student who is struggling with issues related to sexual identity—needs help, advice, or just someone with whom she or he can talk.

The Role and Responsibilities of Safe Staff

1. To be aware of services available to lesbian, gay, bisexual, and transgender (LGBT) youths and adults, including support groups and other community resources.
2. To self-identify in some way as safe staff and thus help students and staff become aware of the services and resources you provide.
3. To help set a climate of safety and support, including the climate as it affects LGBT students, staff, and families (e.g., addressing jokes and name calling when you observe it).
4. To be especially vigilant about areas of the school where safety and support may be especially needed, for example, locker rooms and cafeteria.
5. To invite others to join in creating supportive and safe school climates for LGBT students, staff, and families.
6. To continue learning about the issues affecting LGBT students, staff, and families through asking questions, ongoing conversation with others, reading, and in-services.

Handout 2.2. Attitudes Toward Differences: The Riddle Scale

ATTITUDE	CHARACTERISTIC
Repulsion	People who are different are strange, sick, crazy, and aversive.
Pity	People who are different are somehow born that way and that is pitiful.
Tolerance	Being different is just a phase of development that most people "grow out of."
Acceptance	Implies that one needs to make accommodations for another's differences; does not acknowledge that another's identity may be of the same value as one's own.
Support*	Works to safeguard the rights of those who are different.
Admiration	Acknowledges that being different in our society takes strength.
Appreciation	Values the diversity of people and is willing to confront the insensitive attitudes.
Nurturance	Assumes that the differences in people are indispensable in society.

All educators have a minimal responsibility to be at this level.

Source: Hower, J.A., Bankins, M., and Crahen. S. (1987). *Appreciation of Difference: Riddle Scale of Homophobia*. Paper presented at the meeting of ACPA/NASPA Celebration, Chicago. Scale developed by Dorothy Riddle, PhD.

Handout 2.3. Qualities of a LGBT Ally

An ally to LGBT individuals is a person who:

1. Believes that it is in her or his self-interest to be a friend and supporter of and advocate for LGBT individuals.
2. Has worked to develop an understanding of LGBT issues, and is comfortable with his or her knowledge of gender identity and sexual orientation.
3. Is comfortable saying the words "gay," "lesbian," "bisexual," and "transgender."
4. Understands how patterns of oppression operate, and is willing to identify and challenge oppressive attitudes and behaviors of others.
5. Works to be an ally to all oppressed groups.
6. Is quick to take pride in, and appreciate successes in combating homophobia and heterosexism.
7. Is open (i.e., "comes out of the closet") with his or her pride and support.
8. Chooses to align with LGBT individuals and represents their needs, especially when they are unable to do so themselves.
9. Expects to make some mistakes and does not use the feelings of guilt to become an ineffective ally.
10. Promotes a sense of community with LGBT individuals and teaches others about the importance of such an alliance. Encourages others to also provide advocacy.
11. Is not afraid to be called the same names and to be harassed in the same ways as those with whom he or she is standing in solidarity.
12. Is able to address/confront bigoted or insensitive individuals without being defensive, sarcastic, or threatening.

Handout 2.4. Homophobia and Heterosexism

homophobia: The irrational fear of a sexual orientation other than heterosexuality. It is expressed as negative feelings, attitudes, or actions against lesbians, gay men, bisexuals, and transgender people. Homophobia also includes the fear of being perceived as lesbian or gay, and the fear of one's own feelings of affection for the same gender.

components of homophobia: Fear of differences; anxiety about sexuality in general and same-sex sensual/sexual feelings and behaviors in particular; and sexism—fear of sex/gender role violation.

internalized homophobia: The belief by LGBT people that same-gender sexuality is inferior to heterosexuality. Such a belief can lead to self-hatred and difficulty with self-acceptance. For some LGBT persons, it is a major result of societal oppression.

heterosexism: The societal assumption and norm that the practices of heterosexuality are the only accepted and sanctioned expressions of human sexuality. Heterosexism presumes that everyone is or should be heterosexual. It is institutionalized in that it sanctions discrimination and the denial of basic human rights for LGBT people.

Handout 2.5. Heterosexism: Another Pillar of the Power Structure

At the root of homophobia is heterosexism, the system of oppression that reinforces the belief in the inherent superiority of heterosexuality and heterosexual relationships—thereby negating the lives of LGBT persons.

Catholic educators should combine heterosexism with all of the other "isms" that are based on prejudice and injustice (e.g., racism, ageism, and classism). Put another way, all persons who suffer injustice because of any of the "isms" represent the marginalized persons whom the Gospel challenges us all to love and to whom it calls us to minister.

When homophobia is viewed in this bigger picture, we can see how it is one more source of the oppression that serves to hold up society's power structure and to keep the powerless downtrodden (see Figure 2.1).

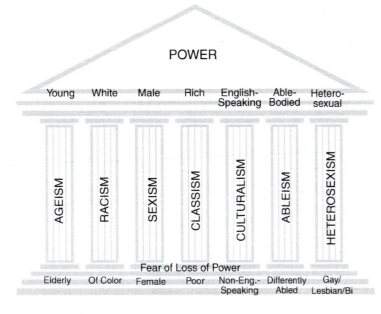

FIGURE 2.1. Heterosexism: Another Pillar of the Power Structure. *Source:* CPCSM. Reprinted with permission.

Handout 2.6. How Homophobia and Heterosexism Hurt Adolescents

Homophobia and heterosexism can negatively impact adolescents—gay and straight—in numerous ways. They can:

1. Lead to an increase in sexual activity as heterosexual teens seek to prove they are not gay/lesbian, and LGBT teens attempt to avoid harassment or to force themselves to change. The consequences of this need to "prove" oneself heterosexually can include promiscuous activity, unwanted pregnancy, and/or contraction of sexual transmitted diseases (STDs).
2. Force teens into rigid gender roles, limiting their aspirations and dreams of what they can be. The consequences of such enforcement can include:
   • Isolation of teens who violate traditional gender roles.
   • Name calling and violence against such teens—heterosexual as well as LGBT.
   • Failure to pursue careers considered nontraditional for one's gender.
3. Force LGBT students to participate in oppression of other LGBT students so as to keep their cover (e.g., they may participate in jokes, name-calling, violence).
4. Make it difficult for heterosexual students to access accurate information about LGBT people. This prevents them from giving their LGBT friends the support they need.
5. Generate fear about expressing physical affection with any same-sex friends. The consequences of such fear are as follows:
   • Intimacy needs go unmet leading to loneliness and isolation.
   • Possible increase in alcohol–drug abuse to provide excuse to be intimate.

*Handout 2.7. Eleven Suggestions for Reducing Homophobia
in Your Environment*

1. *Make no assumption about sexuality.* If a student has not used a pronoun when discussing a relationship, don't assume one. Use neutral language such as "Are you seeing anyone?" instead of "Do you have a boyfriend?" In addition, do not assume that a female student who confides a "crush" on another girl is a lesbian. Labels are often too scary and sometimes not accurate. Let students label themselves.

2. *Have something that is LGBT supportive visible in your classroom/office.* A sticker, a poster, a flyer, a brochure, a book, a button. This will identify you as a safe person to talk to and will hopefully allow a LGBT or questioning youth to break his/her silence.

3. *Support, normalize, and validate students' feelings about their sexuality.* Let them know that you are there for them. If you cannot be supportive, please refer to someone who can be. Then work on your biases by reading, learning, and talking to people who are comfortable with this issue. And always remember: the problem is homophobia not homosexuality.

4. *Do not advise youths to come out to parents, family, and friends, as they need to come out at their own safe pace.* Studies show that a high number of gay youths are forced to leave their home after they tell their parents.* It is their decision and they have to be aware of and be willing to live with the possible consequences. Help them figure out what makes sense for them.

5. *Guarantee confidentiality with students.* Students need to know that their privacy will be respected or they will not be honest about this important issue. If you cannot maintain confidentiality for legal reasons, let students know this in advance.

6. *Challenge homophobia.* As a role model for your students, respond to homophobia immediately and sincerely. Challenge the witnesses of homophobic comments and actions—reminding them that when such words and actions are known to be wrong yet go unchallenged, there are no "innocent bystanders" but passive participants in abusive behavior. Encourage in-service trainings for staff and students on homophobia and its impact on all students.

7. *Combat heterosexism in your classroom.* Include visibly gay and lesbian role models in your classroom and curriculum. Again, use of neutral language is also important. For example, use "spouse" or "partner" instead of "husband" or "wife."

8. *Learn about and refer to community organizations.* Familiarize yourself with resources; make sure they are ongoing so that you can inform the individual being referred as to what kinds of procedures, questions, etc., to expect when he or she contacts a given community organization. Also, become aware of gay-themed bibliographies and refer to gay-positive books.

9. *Encourage school administrators to adopt and enforce antidiscrimination policies for their schools or school systems that include sexual orientation.* The language should be included in all written materials along with race, gender, religion, etc.

(This issue will be explored further in Session 5 "The Classroom Setting and Beyond").

10. *Provide role models.* LGBT and straight students alike benefit from having openly gay teachers, coaches, and administrators. Obviously, in the Catholic setting such openness is not always possible. This is tragic for all concerned, as such role models give straight students an alternative to the inaccurate stereotypes they have received and gay students the opportunity to see healthy LGBT adults. The same is true for straight school faculty and staff. They can model for straight students healthy behavior in their approach to sexual orientation and gender identity

---

* For the most up-to-date figures related to LGBT youths, visit the Web site of the Gay and Lesbian, and Straight Educators Network at www.glsen.org.

issues, and in their sensitive response to LGBT students as well as to all students perceived as "different." Such faculty and staff can also show LGBT students that straight people can learn to be sensitive to their feelings and needs and that LGBT students should not immediately write off straight people as untrustworthy and to be avoided.

11. *Commit yourself to the lifelong process of identifying and facing homophobia within yourself.*

Handout 2.8. Responding to Harassment: Dos and Don'ts

Do deal with the situation immediately.

Don't ignore it, let it pass unchallenged, or let intangible fears block your ability to act.

Do confirm that the particular type of abuse is hurtful and harmful and will not be tolerated.

Do value the feelings of others by active, sensitive listening.

Do take steps to support the victim and enable her or him to develop a stronger sense of self.

Do take those involved aside to discuss the incident.

Do apply consequences to the attacker in accordance with the school rules, code of behavior, and race/ethno-cultural relations policy.

Don't overreact with another put-down of the offender.

Don't impose consequences before finding out exactly what happened from those involved.

Don't focus entirely on applying consequences to the offender while ignoring the feelings of the victim.

Don't humiliate the attacker when imposing consequences. Remember that the attacker may feel like a victim too.

Don't embarrass either party publicly.

Do explain to students why such incidents occur and undertake ongoing long-term (proactive) strategies with the class for combating stereotyping, prejudice, and negative attitudes to differences.

Don't assume that the incident is an isolated occurrence, divorced from the overall context in which it occurred.

READING ASSIGNMENT

(To be distributed at the end of Session 2)

A Teaching Story

A Catholic high school teacher recalls a transforming experience, not only for a brave young woman named Sara, but for all who were open to the authenticity of her "coming out."

I don't think many of us consider classrooms as sacred places. Nor do we imagine being blessed within their walls. We hope for teachable moments, for assignments done well, or perhaps just better than the ones from last month. We hope for a thank-you note for, say, a letter of recommendation, and for times of silence that actually mean something. Many days we hope just to make it through with some purpose and sanity.

Yet once in a while the place we meet our students becomes the ground for something so moving that it shifts the assumptions we brought with us that day and sends us away awakened, edified, and transformed.

I call a moment like this a blessing, and it happened for me one Friday morning in March during my twenty-sixth year of teaching.

During second period, a senior named Sara stood up in front of forty-five or so of her peers and several adults to deliver her "gender project." After requesting the use of a podium and then arranging her folder on top of it, she looked up and confidently faced her audience. She was really going to go through with this I thought, as I watched with both admiration and concern.

When Sara approached me earlier that week, I had asked her, "Do you really want to do this?" It was both excitement and apprehension that fueled my question. Yet I knew that there really wasn't any way to say no to Sara. She had a look in her eye; it was the look of a focused and healthy young woman. I hadn't seen that look reflected in her face for a long time. I sensed very clearly that Sara knew what she needed to do; she was on a mission.

And now as she began her presentation, her voice was quiet but clear and audible. Everyone in the room sensed that something important was about to happen. Some of my colleagues and I, as well as a few of Sara's closest friends, had been tipped to the possibility of what she was about to do.

Sara noted that as part of her "gender project," she had recently talked with three young gay people and one older gay woman, and she proceeded to share the reflections each had offered her. Next she read from a postcard she had found, which listed reasons for supporting gay rights.

As Sara spoke, I scanned the group of young people that comprised her audience. Was there a way to read their thoughts?

I looked at the young woman who, along with her parents, had invited Sara into her house last June. She too was a state-caliber soccer player who thought that rescuing Sara from the cold of her family history would be good for Sara. They'd win a state championship together. Yet she hadn't reckoned on the turmoil: Sara's suicide attempt, her mood swings, the invasion of her space, the friction of sharing close quarters with another person.

Another young woman in the front row was also a teammate of Sara's. She seems sometimes sour, as if life has been cruel to her. What was she thinking?

Part of Sara's presentation involved relating the story of one of the people she had interviewed for her research. This person's name was Shelley, and her high school experiences, as related by Sara, had a profound impact on me: "Mom liked to throw things at us. Her favorite words for me were 'fucking dyke.'"

As Sara recited these words I lowered my head into my hands. I had written Sara a note earlier in the year after she had written a piece about her sordid family history. I remember that October evening as I sat at the dining room table reading her essay. I wanted so much to find her—wherever she was—and give her a big hug. I remember thinking, "No kid deserves this kind of life, especially this one. How could anyone generate this kind of hatred for a beautiful kid like Sara?" It was one of those moments in teaching when you just wonder about the kids who sit in front of you every day, when it hits you that there is pain beneath the lack of motivation, wounded spirits beneath the bravado.

When Sara spoke about an English teacher who hadn't taught Shelley much English but a lot about acceptance of other people, a certain realization began to dawn. Further light was shed when I heard that Shelley, like Sara, had also attempted suicide in her senior year.

As Sara's presentation progressed, I kept waiting for the slightest catch in her voice. Surely with the weight of all she was imparting, there had to come some display of emotion. Yet Sara calmly finished Shelley's story by declaring that she was Shelley; and that she, Sara, was lesbian.

"There are a few gay people in this class," Sara noted, "and a heck of a lot in this school. They are not just 'out there' somewhere else." She then said that she would be glad to talk to anyone about her life and her story, and that if people had a problem with her then they didn't have to talk to her. "Most people I asked about coming out [in the way I just have] were very skeptical, but I figure it won't matter to people who are really my friends. If people react badly, well, I only have two months left here, and I think I can take it." With these words, Sara went back to her seat.

There was applause and then a long silence that no one quite knew how to end. Finally a young woman named Erica spoke up: "I just want you to know that what you just did is one of the bravest things I have ever seen."

When students were told that the class was ended, more than a few gathered around Sara to thank her with words and hugs. I gave her a hug too.

David, a Native American, was one of the students who approached Sara. The handshake he offered her was a supreme, if awkward, gesture of deep respect. Chad, a tall, soft-spoken senior who pitches for the baseball team, later wrote that Sara's presentation had brought tears to his eyes.

I'm still not sure what to make of that morning. As one of the students later wrote in his journal, "I never saw anything like it in my life. She just didn't give a shit what anybody thought." How true! What I also know is that Sara has been a blessing to our school: a transfer student who came in as a soccer star and ended up breaking the long-standing silence about gays and lesbians at our school.

Sara said at one point after her Friday morning presentation that it had seemed a perfect time to come out; everybody had to do a project related to gender; it was third term, and her classmates had gotten to know her as an all-state soccer goalie, a fine student, and friend of many of the class leaders; and finally, and perhaps most important, the secret had been kept long enough: "I remember how much pain I went through and how alone I felt."

After Easter break, I asked Sara whether she would be willing to talk to another class. Her willingness to do so confirmed for me that her coming to terms with her sexuality had made Sara a much healthier person. There are certain events of her childhood and adolescence with which she'll have to struggle for the rest of her life. But her coming out (first to her friend and teammate, Helen, then to her "adopted" parents, other close friends, her brother, and finally, her class) seems to have sparked her energy and given her a sense of purpose. On several occasions she has been approached in the halls at school by students who had heard about what she did and wanted to talk with her about their own questions on sexual identity. She said that those conversations repaid her for the risk she took and would more than make up for any grief she might ever suffer as a result of her coming out.

When Sara gave her speech for the second time, she agreed to add a question and answer session. Someone asked her what it felt like to be out. Sara noted that it felt as if she had been "covered with a layer of goo and shit," but that she was now beginning to pick it off. Another of the questions was quite pointed: "There have been rumors that you are going to prom with your girlfriend. Are you?"

Sara responded in her soft-spoken, almost hesitant but ever-thoughtful manner: "I'm considering it, but I have to think about a lot of things, like how the administration would react. Also, people say that alumni and parents might be unhappy and call the school [to complain]. I have to consider how it would affect this class, too."

Along with the other adults present, I was amazed at the perspicacity of her response. Rarely have I seen an eighteen-year-old mature enough to see so far beyond the boundaries of her own issues and identify the ramifications of her potential actions. Her classmates seemed to be completely behind her with regard her attendance at the school's prom. "She pays tuition just like everybody else who will be attending," they reasoned.

In the following days it became clear that the school's principal and at least one of the assistant principals would be supportive of Sara if she did indeed decide to attend the prom with her girlfriend. The final decision would be hers.

Ultimately Sara decided not to go to the prom. Her best friend and her "adopted parents" had all expressed the sentiment that it would not be good for her to attend. I met with Sara that Monday morning. She was clearly having difficulty with the logic behind the position of her adopted parents and her friend, especially given the support they had shown her during her "coming out" process.

Yet once again I was struck by what a selfless move Sara had chosen to make. I believe that she was in fact ready to attend the prom with her girlfriend; and in so doing, ready to bring down a formidable barrier at our Catholic high school. Yet she was more inclined to consider the sentiments of the people who had literally taken her in off the streets, given her a home, and shown her love.

Some months later, a colleague and friend mentioned a homily he had heard at the inner-city Church he and his family attend. The homilist had suggested the idea of "resurrected" people— people who have been through an experience akin to death and come out the other side with a strength that enables them to do improbable things.

I believe that Sara is a person of the resurrection. She has been to the brink and seen death. Maybe that is where her courage comes from. Regardless, I know she did and continues to do improbable things.

After reading "A Teaching Story," reflect upon and respond to the following questions:

1. In Session 1 we discussed common experiences of LGBT youth along with some "recent research findings concerning LGBT youth." How are some of these experiences and findings reflected in Sara's story?

2. The author maintains that Sara's coming out had made her a much "healthier person." What do you see as evidence for this?

3. Why does the author describe Sara as "a person of the resurrection"? Who are some people in your life that would fit this description? Do you agree that Sara is such a person?

Session 3

Coming Out

In its broadest sense, the term "coming out" is all about growing in awareness and acceptance of oneself. Accordingly, it is not an event, but rather a life-long process. We are all involved in this process as we all grow in awareness of different aspects of our lives.

Topics Explored

- The experience of coming out.
- Recent research findings on LGBT teenagers.
- High risk factors for LGBT youth.
- Professional relationship and boundary issues.
- Responding to LGBT youth in practical and pastorally sensitive ways.

Recommended Equipment/Resources

Masking tape
Easel with pad and markers
Notepads, pens, and pencils
Prayer: "The Light Within" (see Appendix 1)

Handouts

3.1 Coming Out: A Definition
3.2 Stages of Coming Out for LGBT Persons
3.3 High-Risk Factors for LGBT Youth
3.4 Defining Professional Boundaries and Professional Helping Relationships
3.5 General Guidelines for Professional Helping Relationships
3.6 Threats to Professional Helping Relationships
3.7 How to Prevent Boundary Crossings and Violations
3.8 Pastoral Care Tips for Classroom Teachers
3.9 Suggestions for Responding to Youth About LGBT Concerns/Questions

Creating Safe Environments for LGBT Students
© 2007 by The Haworth Press, Inc. All rights reserved.
doi:10.1300/5723_05

Format

1. Facilitator begins Session 3 by sharing the coming-out reflection, "The Light Within" (see Appendix 1) and the following two statements. All three pieces were written by former Catholic high school students.

I knew I was different but I didn't have enough courage to ask anyone about it. I hoped I would change, but it just came natural for me to like other guys. I experienced self-hate because I was gay. It would take many years before I could accept myself as a handiwork of God's creation and realize it was good, that I was good. That pain is what I wish I could save students in our district from. When I was in school, I scoured the dictionary trying to look up words and become educated about what I was experiencing in my own life. I couldn't find any books in the library. I wonder nowadays if kids can find anything in their school libraries.

In the classrooms of my school, teachers would allow students to use words like "faggot" and "dyke," and teachers themselves would even use those words. How could I fully concentrate on my studies and be the student I wanted to be knowing that the adult in the front of the classroom considered people like me worthy of that torment? And on the athletic field coaches I had would say, "You're all playing like a bunch of faggots." Little did my coaches know that their star player was a faggot.

2. Participants briefly discuss the session's opening quotes from LGBT youth and share their thoughts related to the Session 3 Reading Assignment.

3. Revise the term "coming out" by referring to its definition in Handout 1.4 "Human Sexuality Definitions"—"coming out/out of the closet/being out." Terms that one states openly when declaring that one is bisexual, gay, lesbian, or transgender. In contrast, to "stay in the closet" is to hide or deny one's gender identity or sexual orientation either from oneself or from others.

4. Using Handout 3.1 "Coming Out: A Definition," participants discuss the experience and process of "coming out."

5. Participants view and discuss Handout 3.2 "Stages of Coming Out for LGBT Persons."

6. In light of this awareness of coming out, participants briefly revise Handout 1.6 "Recent Research Findings Concerning LGBT Youth in Catholic Schools," and Handout 1.7 "Important Points Concerning Psychosocial Aspects of LGBT Youth." Facilitator notes that given these findings and experiences, certain "high risk factors" for LGBT youth have been identified (Handout 3.3 "High-Risk Factors for LGBT Youth").

7. Facilitator introduces the topic of boundaries and LGBT students by having participants view and discuss Handout 3.4 "Defining Professional Boundaries and Professional Helping Relationships," Handout 3.5 "General Guidelines for Professional Helping Relationships," Handout 3.6 "Threats to Professional Helping Relationships," and Handout 3.7 "How to Prevent Boundary Crossings and Violations."

8. Facilitator elicits responses from participants to the points raised by Handouts 3.4, 3.5, and 3.6. What other insights and recommendations can participants share in relation to professional boundaries and students in need of guidance, support, and affirmation?

9. In light of these shared insights and recommendations and those advanced by Handouts 3.4, 3.5, 3.6, and 3.7, participants in groups of four or five discuss and role-play the following scenarios:

- *In your role as a safe-staff person you have given much support to an emotionally needy LGBT student. One day after class, the student, assuming that as a safe-staff person you yourself are also LGBT, discloses to you that he has developed a crush on you. Further, he says that all of the other LGBT students are too immature for him and he would like to see you socially outside of the school. How do you respond to this student?*
- *On entering your classroom you walk in on a group of students speculating on the sexual orientation of each faculty member. You are known by these students to be heterosexual and they attempt to engage you in their game, coaxing you to share about the private lives of*

other teachers. Do you let this pass as innocent tomfoolery or do you challenge these students? How do you justify your decision?

- *You are a closeted LGBT teacher. You're closeted out of fear of losing your job. You're also a very popular teacher—one whom many LGBT students seek out for guidance. Recently, a few students, who have begun to trust you with more personal information, respectfully ask you about your sexual orientation. They state that your support would be more credible if they knew that you could truly identify with the struggles they are dealing with. Do you share your orientation with them? Why or why not?*

- *Your school is in the middle of an assembly in which a new antiharassment policy regarding LGBT students is announced. In the middle of this announcement you observe several students start to cry and then suddenly depart from the hall. Do you pursue them right then or at a later time and ask them about the source of their distress? Or do you let this incident pass, telling yourself that is none of your business? How do you justify your response?*

- *In the fall of the school year a student comes out to you and seems at peace with her decision. You support her in the decision and tell her that your door is always open for further discussion. However it's nearing Christmas break and you've not heard from her since your first discussion. Also, you have seen the student in the hall on a number of recent occasions and each time she looks troubled and dejected. What do you do? Why?*

10. Facilitator notes that there are practical (and pastorally sensitive) guidelines for responding to LGBT youth—guidelines that contain valuable strategies in the event of a LGBT youth sharing information about awareness and/or concerns about his or her sexual orientation, or of a student simply asking questions about sexual orientation in general. These guidelines reflect the "pastoral mandate" discussed in Session 1 "Laying the Foundations."

Handout 3.6, for instance, offers pastoral care tips by and for classroom teachers. Handout 3.8 contains guidelines developed by a Catholic high school teacher for responding to youth around LGBT questions/concerns.

Facilitator elicits responses from participants to the suggestion/guidelines offered by both Handout 3.6 and Handout 3.9. Have participants other guidelines to add? Would some be difficult to follow in certain situations or school communities? Why? How could these difficulties be overcome?

11. In light of these guidelines, and with awareness of the "high-risk factors" for LGBT youth and the negative impact of homophobia and heterosexism explored in the previous session, participants in groups of four or five engage in discussion and role-play that focuses on the following scenarios:

- *A bright but somewhat naive student has just come out during a project in one of your classes. In his newfound exuberance he shares with you that he is tired of living in denial of his sexual orientation and now must be honest and let everyone in the school know who he really is. You know that there are a number of significant safety issues that he has not at all addressed in his school. You are very concerned for his safety and he does not seem to comprehend the risks. What do you do? Why?*

- *A student who is a "star athlete" has recently come out to you. She feels the need to share her secret with other faculty members whom she perceives to be sensitive to the issue. She has great respect for her basketball coach who is very popular, and the student wants to tell him. You have firsthand knowledge that the coach is very homophobic. What do you do? Why?*

- *A seventeen-year-old senior student recently came out to you. He also revealed to you that he finds the other LGBT students he knows to be "too immature," and that he has been*

sneaking into a gay bar downtown with a fake ID, going home with much older men, and engaging in unsafe sex with them. Do you intervene in this situation? If so, how and why?
- *There is a female student in your class who is considered a lesbian by other class members. You happen to know that this young woman has been acting out in a sexually promiscuous manner in an attempt to deny her real same-sex feelings and to divert attention away from her sexual orientation. You are very concerned that she might become pregnant if this behavior continues. One day after class she takes you aside and asks you about available birth control. You interpret this as a veiled cry for help. Do you intervene? Why or why not? If so, how?*

12. To conclude Session 3, facilitator distributes Session 4 Reading Assignment to participants and asks that for the next session they read and reflect upon the anecdotal pieces that comprise this assignment.

Handout 3.1. Coming Out: A Definition

In its broadest sense, the term "coming out" is all about growing into awareness and acceptance of oneself. Accordingly, it is not an event, but rather a lifelong process. We are all involved in this process as we grow in awareness of different aspects of our lives. We grow in awareness and acceptance of our need for human relationships, our mortality, of the feminine and masculine dimensions of our personality, of our connectedness with each other and the environment, and of our own and others' strengths and limitations.

For the majority of people, awareness and acceptance of their sexuality is affirmed and encouraged by society and the Church. This is not always the case with people who are gay, lesbian, bisexual, or transgender. For these individuals, "coming out" to their sexuality—to themselves and to others—can be a long, painful, even dangerous process.

Handout 3.2. Stages of Coming Out for LGBT Persons

The following framework for understanding the stages of coming out was designed by Warren J. Blumenfeld and included in his article "Adolescence, Sexual Orientation and Identity: An Overview." This article was published online from 1994 to 1998 by the Gay and Lesbian and Straight Educators Network (GLSEN).

Blumenfeld's framework is a synthesis of three theoretical models charting the coming out process proposed by Richard R. Troiden, Vivienne Cass, and Eli Coleman. These researchers pattern their theories on the multistage models of personality development pioneered by sociologist Charles Horton Cooley, philosopher George Herbert Mead, and psychoanalysts Sigmund Freud and Erik Erikson—all of whom believed that personal identity develops along an interactive process between the individual and his or her environment.

When exploring this or any other framework that seeks to map out the experience of coming out, it is important to be mindful of Blumenfeld's insight:

> Each person comes out in different ways under unique circumstances. Studies suggest that the coming-out journey that begins with an early awareness of feelings of difference to the development of an integrated identity takes many years. Some people move more quickly than others. And some may become stuck and never progress to the final stages. The reasons why people move from stage to stage, or fail to move, are very complex. Theorists have stressed, however, that societal attitudes are important in affecting the development of a person's positive identity. (Ojeda, 2003)

Stage 1: Sensitization/Insight

- Usually occurs before puberty and experienced as indistinct feelings of "differentness," which serve as basis for emerging self-perceptions as gay or lesbian in early adolescence.
- Can be viewed as a pre–coming-out stage. Child usually not consciously aware of same-sex feelings or thoughts even though some feelings of sexual attraction begin at ages nine to eleven.
- Since same-sex attractions are vague and weak, and as society's pressures for opposite-sex attractions are strong, the child is not yet ready or willing to label him or herself as gay or lesbian.

Stage 2: Identity Confusion/Isolation

- Usually occurs in early adolescence and may last one month, one year, or indefinitely. This stage is characterized by inner turmoil and uncertainty about sexual identity. A strong self-perception as gay or lesbian has not yet been developed, yet at the same time there is a strong sense of uncertainty about being heterosexual.
- *Individuals at this stage of coming out are confused by:*
  - —Feelings of being sexually different.
  - —Experiences of strong homosexual arousal and behavior.
  - —Societal stigma, which fuels guilt, secrecy, and makes it difficult to meet and interact positively with other LGBT individuals.
  - —Inaccurate knowledge about what it means to be gay or lesbian.

- *Sudden awareness of a "terrible secret" can cause many intense negative feelings—fear, dread, guilt, shame, depression, isolation, and alienation. Response to inner dissonance is manifested in one or more of the following stigma-management strategies (often forms of internalized homophobia):*
  1. Denial of homosexual component of feelings, fantasies or behaviors ("It's just a phase," "I was just drunk . . .").
  2. Attempts to change or alter their same-sex orientation (e.g., psychotherapy).
  3. Many forms of avoidance:
     —Stopping behaviors and interests associated with LGBT identity
     —Dating or avoiding opposite-sex persons
     —Limiting exposure to positive information
     —Telling homophobic jokes, gay-bashing
     —Drugs and alcohol, running away, promiscuity, suicide
  4. Acceptance of same-sex feelings, fantasies, and behavior and the seeking out of more information and support, leads to a diminishing sense of isolation.

Stage 3: Identity Tolerance/Disclosure

- At this stage the individual comes to acknowledge to himself or herself and others (usually other gays/lesbians or trusted heterosexual adults first) that he or she is "probably" gay/lesbian.
- Individual begins to experiment sexually and explore LGBT culture. A positive gay/lesbian identity begins to emerge.
- Usually individuals are now ready for support group, or to ask a gay/lesbian person out on a date.
- Usually individuals also begin living "double lives"—seeking out other LGBT persons while still passing as straight in other important areas of their lives.
- Can be a risky time for teenagers to make impulsive decisions to "go public." They can benefit from much guidance at this stage—as consequences and safety must be considered.

Stage 4: Identity Acceptance/Socialization

- Marked by acceptance, not merely tolerance of LGBT self-image.
- Venturing further into LGBT cultures, serving to validate and normalize their sexual identity as way of life.
- Same-sex love relationships and friendships with adult LGBT persons. LGBT role models develop.
- Might make public LGBT identity by attending a public event (e.g., Pride Parade). Might still limit contact with family and heterosexual peers to avoid confrontations.

Stage 5: Identity Pride/Commitment

- Marked by confidence in LGBT identity tempered by awareness of society's prejudices. Solid commitment to LGBT community is made—one that fosters a strong sense of belonging.

- Public identity brought in line with private identity—less energy spent concealing identity and more energy spent defending homosexuality as an acceptable and normal way of life.
- A "gay and proud," sexual identity becomes an important aspect of life; political activism and defiance of heterosexual conventions might also increase.
- Being LGBT now becomes not only accepted but even becomes preferred to heterosexuality.

Stage 6: Identity Synthesis

- Integration of LGBT identity into all elements of life. It is now viewed as just one of many elements in the definition of self.
- Similarities with straight peers are recognized and contact with them seems less threatening as LGBT individual now feels confident enough of his or her identity to come out to the world.

Handout 3.3. High-Risk Factors for LGBT Youth

Harassment and Violence at School

A 1998 survey of fifty-eight high schools conducted by the Massachusetts Department of Education revealed that 22 percent of gay respondents had skipped school in the past month because they felt unsafe. Thirty-one percent had been threatened or injured at school sometime during the previous twelve months. Such statistics prompted *In These Times* magazine to declare in 2001 that "persecution of gay high school students, and students perceived to be gay, [is] endemic."

In June 2001, Human Rights Watch released a 203-page report entitled "Hatred in the Hallways: Violence and Discrimination Against Lesbian, Gay, Bisexual and Transgender Students in U.S. Schools." The report suggests that gay teenagers in U.S. schools are often subjected to such intense bullying that they are unable to receive an adequate education. It is a problem, the report says, that affects as many as 2 million school-age youth nationwide.

Anthony Chase writing on the Human Rights Watch report for *In These Times,* notes that "schools typically act as if this phenomenon does not exist." Furthermore, "school officials usually ignore such harassment . . . tormentors are often not held accountable, and . . . in some cases, school officials have encouraged or participated in the abuse."

Chase reports that "Beth Reis, a principal researcher of a study of school-related anti-gay violence in Washington State, observed that harassment, if not ignored, is typically dismissed as 'teasing.' Sometimes the victims are advised that if they insist upon being openly gay, they have to expect such treatment." Joyce Stanton Mitchell reports in *College Board Review* that a survey of the nation's forty-two largest school districts indicates that 76 percent do not provide teacher training on issues facing gay students. Indeed, teachers ignore instances of antigay harassment 97 percent of the time.

Negative Impact of Harassment on LGBT Students' Academic Performance and College Ambitions

A 2000 GLSEN study found that 78 percent of students reported hearing antigay remarks and/or other forms of harassment every day in school. Key Findings of GLSEN's 2003 National School Climate Survey are as follows:

1. *Unchecked harassment correlates with poor performance and diminished aspirations.* LGBT youth who report significant verbal harassment are twice as likely to report that they do not intend to go on to college and their GPAs are significantly lower (2.9 versus 3.3).

2. *Supportive teachers can make a difference.* LGBT students (24.1 percent), who cannot identify supportive faculty, report that they have no intention of going to college. That figure drops to just 10.1 percent when LGBT students can identify supportive staff at their school.

3. *Policymakers have an opportunity to improve school climates.* LGBT students who did not have (or did not know of) a policy protecting them from violence and harassment were nearly 40 percent more likely to skip school because they were simply too afraid to go.

4. *Harassment continues at unacceptable levels and is too often ignored.* Eighty-four percent of LGBT students report being verbally harassed because of their sexual orientation. Around 82.9 percent of students report that faculty never or rarely intervene when present.

Other Negative Impacts of Harassment

- LGBT youth often feel forced to tell or laugh at LGBT jokes. This can compound feelings of low self-esteem and self-hatred.
- Unmet needs for love and acceptance can lead to social and emotional isolation and to a life-long pattern of compulsive sexual acting out in search of love.
- The negative, self-destructive impact of harassment can also be directed outward. Reporter Anthony Chase (*In These Times,* July 9, 2001) notes that in August 1999, four months after Eric Harris and Dylan Klebold went on a shooting spree, killing thirteen people and wounding twenty-three at their high school in Littleton, Colorado, Dave Cullen of Salon reported that the two youths "had endured repeated harassment due to rumors they were gay. Jocks especially taunted the pair with epithets like 'faggot' and 'homo'" (online at http://www.salon.com/news/feature/1999/04/27/gay/index.html).
- Such a revelation led Chase to investigate other high school shootings. The findings of his research are disturbing:
  - —On February 2, 1996, fourteen-year-old Barry Loukaitis killed a teacher and two students at Frontier Junior High School in Moses Lake, Washington. He had been taunted by school jocks who said he was a "faggot."
  - —On October 1, 1997, sixteen-year-old Luke Woodham killed two students and wounded seven others at Pearl High School in Pearl, Mississippi. He had often been called "gay" by classmates.
  - —On December 1, 1997, fourteen-year-old Michael Carneal killed three students and wounded five others at Heath High School in West Paducah, Kentucky. He had actually been called "gay" in the school newspaper. His mother was distressed at the lack of concern among school authorities when she complained.
  - —The pattern has held in the attacks subsequent to Columbine as well. In March 2001, after continuous torment by school mates, fifteen-year-old Charles "Andy" Williams, a boy reportedly preoccupied with Harris and Klebold, opened fire at Santana High school in Santee, California, shooting fifteen students and adults and killing two. He had been derided by classmates for being a "skinny faggot."

Suicide

- In August 2001 findings related to the National Survey on Adolescent Sexual Orientation and Suicide Risk—the first national study on gay teen suicide risk—were published in the *American Journal of Public Health.* The survey's main conclusion was that "sexual minority youths are more likely than their peers to think about and attempt suicide" (Russell and Joyner, 2001).

Among the study's findings were the following:

- Gay and bisexual teens are more than twice as likely to be suicidal as their straight counterparts.
- Fifteen percent of youth with an attraction toward the same sex had considered or attempted suicide.
- Gay teens are more likely to be depressed, and likely to abuse alcohol and drugs.

Soon after the publication of the survey's findings, Stephen T. Russell, PhD, of the Department of Human and Community Development at the University of California and co-author of the study, expressed the hope that something could be done for at-risk sexual minority teens.

The survey that Russell and colleague Kara Joyner conducted showed that gay teens are more likely to be depressed and abuse alcohol and drugs. Depression and substance abuse are both considered risk factors for suicide in all teens.

- Writing for *In These Times* magazine in July 2001, Anthony Chase notes that "gay males account for more than half of male youth suicide," and identifies "a pivotal 1978 study by Alan P. Bell and Martin Weinberg of Indiana University [which] first indicated a suicide rate among homosexual males 14 times higher than that of their heterosexual peers." Study after study," notes Chase, "reconfirms this result."

Seattle Schools' 1995 Youth Risk Behavior Survey (www.virtualcity.com/youthsuicide/news/seattle.htm), for instance, aimed to examine the "homosexuality factor in the suicidality statistical results." Some of its finding included the following:

- Gay- or bisexual-identified adolescents and heterosexual-identified adolescents assumed or suspected of being homosexually oriented (and thus subjected to verbal abuse, with a likelihood of physical abuse) are at about equal risk to be suicide attempters: 20.5 percent and 20.3 percent. Yet they are about four times more at risk for a suicide attempt than heterosexual-identified adolescents not targeted for such abuse.
- Adolescents targeted for antigay abuse accounted for 21.3 percent of suicide attempters, and 27.8 percent of suicide attempters who required/sought medical attention in association with their suicide attempt.

The authors of the survey also related the following:

One lesbian youth interviewed reported [that] being told she was a lesbian was [like] jerking her out of a psychological "closet" before she was ready to recognize and accept this fact about herself. Therefore, her suicide attempt (requiring medical attention) was more related to not wanting to be what she was repeatedly told she was: a lesbian. Many gay males report that they were also defined to be gay or "a fag" well before they knew what it meant, and well before they were ready to accept this fact about themselves. Therefore, a significant percentage of adolescents who reported being "heterosexual" and having attempted suicide may eventually identify as gay or bisexual and, if studied again, the associated "suicide attempt" data would then be in the "gay/bisexual" category. (Reis and Saewyc, 1999)

Handout 3.4. Defining Professional Boundaries and Professional Helping Relationships

Professional boundaries:

- Are the limits that allow for a safe relationship with students based on their needs?
- Produce consistency and predictability in behavior
- Define how power is exercised within the professional helping relationship
- Protect both the student and the professional helper within the relationship

Characteristics of a professional helping relationship are as follows:

- A professional helping relationship is a professional relationship based on trust
- There is a clear understanding that the student is vulnerable
- There is a necessary power differential between helping professional and the student

The power differential in a professional helping relationship is as follows:

- The student has needs and the helping professional has the resources
- The helper has access to the student's personal and academic data
- The student is vulnerable
- There is potential for abuse of the student through abuse of the power possessed by the helping professional. Accordingly, there is need for the student's protection.

Handout 3.5. General Guidelines for Professional Helping Relationships

- Confidentiality is crucial and of paramount importance as the foundation of professional integrity and to engender trusting relationships with students seeking our help.
- The top priority is the needs of the student, not of the helping professional. It is inappropriate and unethical for the helping professional to satisfy his or her personal needs (e.g., the need to be needed, to be "cool," to be a "buddy," to satisfy romantic/sexual needs). It is important for the professional to have sources of support, affirmation, and fulfillment in his or her private/social life.
- To be "professional" does not mean the teacher/counselor should behave in a detached, cold, and uninvolved manner, or mean that he or she does not stop caring for the student. Nevertheless, professional teachers/counselors do not get so involved with students that they can no longer be helpful.
- As helping professionals we need to keep in mind whose needs or problems we are dealing with and who has the responsibility for their solution. We should not do for others that which they can and should do for themselves.
- It is still a great service to be "just" a caring adult and a healthy role model—one cannot, for example, be a parent and undo all of the student's traumas and make up for all his or her deprivations. Minority students—including LGBT students—and students from troubled families may have many additional needs. Caring and helping professionals need to know when such students require professional help above and beyond what they can provide, and where such help can be accessed.
- Helping professionals need to be ready for students to test their limits. Limit setting is the responsibility of the helping professionals.
- Identity development is a vulnerable time for all students, especially regarding romantic, emotional, and sexual feelings and needs. Helping professionals need to be aware of attempts by students to make them into a hero/heroine (e.g., "You're the only one who cares about me; the only one I can turn to for help.").
- Do not make promises you cannot keep. For example, "I'll always be there for you." "You can call me anytime." "There's nothing I won't do for you."
- Helping professionals need to remember that it is their responsibility to enforce boundaries. They must refer to another staff person if they are unable to do so for some reason.
- Helping professionals should always consult with colleagues for feedback about adherence to these guidelines. This is not a sign of weakness or incompetence, but a professional duty and an essential component in all helping professions.

Handout 3.6. Threats to Professional Helping Relationships

1. Boundary crossings

   - Boundary crossings are brief excursions across boundaries with a return to established limits of the professional relationship.
   - They may begin as a simple act of kindness or courtesy. They may be intentional or unintentional.
   - They usually have no harmful long-term effects.

2. Boundary violations

   - *Boundary violations are characterized by:*
     —Role reversal and secrecy.
     —Indulgence of personal privilege by the professional.
     —Personal rather than professional relationship.
     —Potential for devastating long-term effects.

3. Professional sexual misconduct

   - Is defined as an overt or covert expression of erotic or romantic thoughts/feelings/gestures by a professional toward a student. These expressions are sexual or may be reasonably construed as sexual.
   - Is usually intentional.
   - May or may not begin with other boundary violations.
   - Parallels incest experience.
   - Long-term future effects may not be readily apparent in the present.

Handout 3.7. How to Prevent Boundary Crossings and Violations

- Always follow the "Golden Rule" of professional boundaries: Do or say nothing in private or public that cannot be documented in the student's file or that cannot be shared with colleagues.
- Helping professionals need to always remember that they are the ones responsible for establishing and maintaining appropriate boundaries, and for keeping the focus on the student and the student's needs.
- Helping professionals need to remain aware and reflective about themselves and other staff. For example, they should be open to asking themselves: With which students and in what situations am I vulnerable?
- An atmosphere of mutual trust and help among fellow colleagues is important to foster. Within this atmosphere, professionals should feel free to:
  —Share their vulnerabilities and give permission for feedback.
  —Respect feelings of discomfort about their own and other colleagues' interactions with students.
  —Be unafraid to confront each other and not be defensive when confronted.
  —Have a life of their own so as to meet their own personal needs.

Handout 3.8. Pastoral Care Tips for Classroom Teachers

1. Be open to learning more about adolescent development, gay and lesbian persons and their experiences, issues of sexuality, and the Church's teaching on such topics.
2. Confront discriminatory comments and behaviors in your classroom and your school. Educate yourself on your school's sexual harassment policy and actively enforce the policy in your dealings with students and staff.
3. Be willing to acknowledge and process your own attitudes of discrimination and prejudice. Find a trusted colleague/s who can provide a forum for open and honest discussion.
4. Trying to guess a person's sexual identity simply feeds into stereotypes that often do injustice to people. Avoid making assumptions about one's sexual orientation.
5. Find ways to incorporate the topic of LGBT people into the curriculum.
6. Remember that you have dealt with gay and lesbian persons in the past. You may not have been aware of their orientation, but chances are you have had comfortable and respectful interactions with these persons.
7. If a youth "comes out" to you, appreciate his or her trust in you and respect the risk he or she is taking (see Handout 3.9). Treat his or her story with confidentiality and make referrals, if necessary (as you would with any student and any issue). It may be that the person simply wishes to share his or her story.
8. Have visible signs in your classroom or office that indicate a supportive and open environment.
9. Be patient with yourself and others—we are all on this journey together.

Handout 3.9. Suggestions for Responding to Youth About LGBT Questions/Concerns

A Catholic high school teacher offers six guidelines for responding to a student when he or she comes out as LGBT or is simply questioning his or her sexual orientation/identity.

1. Be conscious of how knowledgeable and comfortable you are with the subject of homosexuality. Are you willing and able to address/clarify any concerns, questions, or misinformation about homosexuality that the student may express in his or her disclosure?
2. Be aware of both the courage and fear involved in this type of disclosure. Acknowledge this and thank the student for trusting you. Avoid projecting any of your own issues when responding to the student. Remember, any disclosure by a student is always about the student and his or her journey.
3. Assess for any danger that the student may be in, for example, is he/she experiencing suicidal thoughts or attempts? Are there signs of substance abuse? Does he or she seem isolated and/or depressed? Does he or she look to be in poor health? The context of the student's disclosure/questioning may also serve to alert you to any dangers. Has the student raised the issue during class discussion in the presence of others or has he/she sought you out for a private conversation? In the case of the latter, it may mean that it is a more serious issue for the student.
4. Be prepared to use language such as "questioning orientation," if the student appears uncomfortable with terms such as "homosexual," "gay," or "lesbian." Don't assume that any student is willing and/or able to self-identify with regard to sexual orientation.
5. Ask the student with whom he or she has shared this information. Also ascertain who the student would consider as his or her support people. Regardless of whether members of the student's family are identified as part of his or her support network, be aware of the family's role and of any particular cultural issues.
6. Refrain from asking whether the student is romantically involved with someone. If the student offers this information, honor it. But do not ask for it. Such questioning, though done with good intentions, could be misinterpreted.

READING ASSIGNMENT

(To be distributed at end of Session 3)

An Archbishop Addresses LGBT Issues

In April 1998, Archbishop John R. Roach of the archdiocese of St. Paul/Minneapolis, gave the keynote address in the first of a series of luncheon talks sponsored by CPCSM and focused on ministry to LGBT persons. Following are extracts from an article about this event originally published in CPCSM's *Rainbow Spirit* journal.

The archbishop's talk, titled "A Bishop's Journey with Gay Ministry: Transforming Gospel Values into Human Rights and a More Inclusive Church," addressed both the theological basis of ministry to LGBT persons and the fundamental pastoral question: "What do we as Church do in order to make real a sense of compassion, justice and respect for the human dignity of all people?"

> The Catholic Church recognizes and affirms the human dignity and worth of gay men, lesbians, bisexuals and transgender [LGBT] persons . . . they have a right to their own human rights . . . human dignity and rights are God given. They're not earned by our behavior nor are they brought into existence by the power of law.

> Some persons . . . find themselves to be homosexual in orientation through no fault of their own, and our Catholic tradition affirms the human dignity and worth of those persons and recognizes the need for protection of their basic human rights. Like all persons they have a right to respect, economic and personal security, and social equality. It is a matter of injustice when they suffer violation of their basic human rights as a result of prejudice.

> Social isolation, ridicule, and economic deprivation are incompatible with basic social justice and absolutely foreign to our basic sense of decency and to our commitment to the gospel of Jesus Christ.

Yet the archbishop also reminded those present that the Church's moral teaching does not sanction homosexual acts. "That's where our tension is," he said. "We would be foolish not to recognize that theologically and pastorally." Such tensions can be made bearable and even lead to growth, the archbishop noted, when we remember that in all our difficulties "we share a part of the passion, death and resurrection of Jesus. We need to be reminded that you and I are brothers and sisters in the Body of Christ. That has to be the very foundation, the base of the way in which we relate to one another."

Accordingly, the archbishop was adamant that "prejudicial attitudes, discriminatory behaviors and vicious attacks upon persons not only violate the rights of [LGBT] persons but are serious sins against the community of the Church." Throughout his talk, the archbishop praised the work of many in attendance who actively seek to "create an environment of justice, peace, dignity and respect," and who aim to change hearts and attitudes.

> In our pastoral ministry, you and I do everything we possibly can in order to make the community of the Church a community of justice, a community of concern, a community of love. We help people to change their hearts. We make an impact, a difference in our society.

The archbishop noted that the statement of the U.S. Catholic Bishops, *Always Our Children,* offers ways by which we can help move and change hearts. The document, noted the archbishop, is "the outstretched hand of the Church in the United States to help people accept pain in their lives and to give them an understanding of the worth of the individual and the respect that is due to the child of God."

The archbishop stressed that like all gifts from God, sexuality can be channeled toward good or evil. "You are not positioned or moved toward evil because of sexual orientation," the archbishop said. "You can be good or you can be evil with either [heterosexual or homosexual] orientation. All people regardless of orientation, are called to a higher standard of living—one that includes chastity expressed in modesty and self-control.

The archbishop concluded his talk by making a number of pastoral recommendations to parents of gay individuals and to those who minister to them. He called parents to accept and love themselves as parents in order to accept and love their son or daughter, to not blame themselves for their child's sexual orientation, and to do everything possible to continue demonstrating love for their child.

Addressing church ministers, the archbishop called for individuals and support services to be readily available for LGBT persons and their families. Such support groups are "essential," the archbishop noted.

Welcoming homosexuals into the faith community—making special efforts to do so—was also stressed. "Use [LGBT-focused] terms in honest and accurate ways from the pulpit—thus giving others permission to talk about homosexual issues," the archbishop said.

Commenting on the best way to reach out to LGBT youth in high schools, the archbishop expressed his belief that "we have to have our teachers and counselors in our Catholic high schools really committed to the spirit of *Always Our Children,* and do all that we possibly can to be of assistance to parents. It is another form of pastoral ministry."

In his closing remarks, Archbishop Roach reiterated his belief that there is "no complicated theology" necessary in responding to LGBT issues, but instead "the most elemental kind—respect and love for God's people. It's that simple." On the Church's pastoral ministry to LGBT persons, the archbishop noted that "we have and we will continue to get better."

After reading "An Archbishop Addresses LGBT Issues," reflect upon and respond to the following questions:

1. How does the archbishop understand the origins of sexual orientation? Does he, for instance, suggest that sexual orientation is chosen by an individual?

2. Where lies "the tension," according to the archbishop?

3. In what ways do you see safe staff training as creating that "environment of justice, peace, dignity and respect" that the archbishop speaks about?

4. In becoming a safe staff person, how do you see yourself changing hearts and attitudes, making an impact and a difference in our society? How do you relate this to your Christian faith?

5. What aspects of the archbishop's address do you relate to? Are there aspects that challenge you? Please consider sharing these at the beginning of Session 4.

Is God Homophobic?

A Catholic high school student wrestles with a disturbing question.

Among heterosexuals and homosexuals alike, there is a common misconception that the Catholic Church promotes and purveys unequivocal intolerance toward homosexuality. And while the legacy of the Church's intolerance has not gone unwarranted, the Catholic Church does promote tolerance toward all of God's children regardless of their sexual orientation.

However, something that needs to be addressed is the discrepancy between "homosexuality" and "homosexual acts" as designated by the Catholic Church. Pertaining to homosexual acts, the Church continues to toe the line of "love the sinner, hate the sin." This is a good rule of thumb when applying moral standards of judgment universally; however, to use this philosophy in this situation invariably creates a double standard and sends a mixed message to homosexual Catholics.

The Church states that homosexuals "do not choose their condition" because they are either genetically or psychologically predisposed by God to be that way. The Church also says that homosexual acts "under no circumstances can be approved." To assume that God created homosexuals to "abstain from all sexual acts" because such acts are "closed to the gift of life" is unrealistic and unfair. This theological doctrine polarizes homosexual Catholics into a paradox: although the Church to which they belong says it's okay to be gay because that's the way God created them, this same Church places an extremely negative connotation on the way homosexuals express their love for one another. I believe that God created all of us, heterosexual and homosexual alike, to be sexual creatures.

Another issue that surrounds the Church's mixed message is the attitude of heterosexuals within the Church toward Catholic homosexuals. Although the Catholic Church says that we should tolerate homosexuals—in agreement with the universal Christian maxims of peace, love, and understanding that we learned at a young age—the Church inadvertently fosters homophobia by branding as sinners homosexuals who engage in homosexual acts. This equivocating only allows room for Catholics heterosexuals to rationalize their homophobic tendencies. It confronts many of us with a precarious question: How are we, as heterosexual Catholics, supposed to minister to homosexual Catholics within our community?

I feel very strongly about the main principles of Catholicism, yet when it comes to rules on sexuality, I side with those believing that the Church must offer more constructive solutions to the many questions relating to sexual morality. If God created homosexuals to be the way they are, it serves as strong evidence that God did not create sexual acts to be used exclusively for procreation, but as an expression of love and unity between two people.

The Catholic Church is right to take a stance of tolerance toward homosexuals. However, something needs to be done to alleviate the current situation. The Church needs to address the question of how to foster a welcoming environment for homosexuals, and how to create the environment wherein Catholic homosexuals are not forced to compromise their faith for the reality of their lives.

After reading "Is God Homophobic?", reflect upon and respond to the following questions:

1. According to the Catholic high school student who wrote this article, what is the "paradox" that polarizes homosexual Catholics? What is the author's response to such a paradox? What is yours?

2. Do you agree with the author when he states that the Catholic Church "inadvertently fosters homophobia by branding as sinners, homosexuals who engage in homosexual acts"? How does this statement relate to the author's chosen title for his or her article?

3. What are the main differences between this article and the first one you read?

Safe Schools, Sexuality, and Institutional Church Teaching: A Catholic Parent's Perspective

Creating a safe and respectful school environment for all students is not about "sex education." Our efforts do, however, understand sexuality as an integral component of the human person. In that sense, sexuality is at the heart of the work that has to be done. Accordingly, we cannot sidestep the problems that certain ways of understanding Church teaching present for gay, lesbian, bisexual, and transgender (LGBT) persons.

Intimacy needs require attention at every stage of life—including infancy and elder age. In adolescence there are very important development tasks to be addressed. Discovering to whom our sexual energies are directed happens fairly spontaneously, especially if they are directed toward the opposite sex.

For some LGBT youth it may occur just as spontaneously but with greater complications. These complications are the result of societal conditioning and cultural patterns, and they necessitate adult support, nonjudgment, and compassion.

A second task involves making responsible choices around the expression of these intimacy needs. It is essential that clear and loving messages be sent by adults, and vital that encouragement is given for the development of healthy same-sex friendships and affectional relationships.

We need only look at the incidences of harassment and violence directed toward those perceived to be gay and the frequency of LGBT self-destructive acts to glimpse the prison of hostility that surrounds them. Far from encouraging genital activity, a safe and healthy social environment reduces that possibility.

What cannot be ignored is that most homosexual teens, like most heterosexual teens, anticipate loving, long-term relationships that involve sexual expression. The burden of the institutional Church's insistence that homosexual relationships can never include a sexual dimension is so onerous that it must be challenged.

Similarly, the oppressive impact of such a stance must also alert us to its flawed theological underpinnings. Binding an entire population to lifelong celibacy without their input or consent, and declaring that it is ordained by a loving God, is nothing less than abusive—and dismissive of the presence of the divine within all.

The theological basis of this position is riddled with internal illogic. We need to reclaim that basic tenet of spirituality that proclaims and celebrates the goodness of all of God's creation. Intrinsic to this is the acknowledgment that sexual orientation is a fundamental dimension of one's personhood. We, therefore, cannot encumber individuals with proscriptions that deny the inherent goodness of their sexuality.

What might a newly reclaimed spiritual and theological approach to human sexuality—and thus sexual orientation—look like? One hopeful approach that has been offered is by psychologist and Franciscan nun, Fran Ferder. "The hallmark of sexual holiness is not sexual abstinence," she writes, "it is reverence in relationships" (Ferder and Heagle, 2002). Such a statement entails viewing sexual sin not as illicit pleasure but as violation of persons.

LGBT teens deserve the same aspirations as their straight counterparts. They—and their straight counterparts—need to be able to applaud the lived experience of many of today's families grounded in the intimate relationship of longevity between same-sex couples.

LGBT and straight teens alike ought to be able to rejoice that children are often the fruit of these families. Only then will we appreciate the abundance of the love of God and how wondrous is the variety in which our God has made us—each one of us.

Darlene White

After reading "Safe Schools, Sexuality, and Institutional Church Teaching—A Catholic Parent's Perspective," reflect upon and respond to the following questions:

1. What are the two tasks that Darlene White sees as important for those seeking to create safe and respectful school environments?

2. What do you think compels this Catholic parent to challenge the institutional Church's insistence that homosexual relationships can never include a sexual dimension?

3. With which aspect/s of Darlene's article do you relate? Are there aspects that challenge you? Please consider sharing these at the beginning of Session 4.

Session 4

The LGBT Reality and the Catholic Church

To assume that God created homosexuals to "abstain from all sexual acts" because such acts are "closed to the gift of life" is unrealistic and unfair. This theological doctrine polarizes homosexual Catholics into a paradox: the Church to which they belong says that it's okay to be gay because that's the way God created them. Yet this same Church places an extremely negative connotation on the way homosexuals express their love for one another. I believe that God created all of us, heterosexual and homosexual alike, to be sexual creatures.

Catholic High School Student

Topics Explored

- The importance of context.
- The Bible and homosexuality.
- The range of Church teaching related to homosexual orientation and behavior.
- History and ongoing development of the Catholic Church's understanding of human sexuality.
- The Church's pastoral mandate with regard to homosexuality, and how this mandate shapes our approach as high school educators to the interrelated issues of LGBT youth, human sexuality, and sexual orientation.

Recommended Equipment/Resources

Easel with pad and markers
Notepads, pens, and pencils
Masking tape
Prayer: "A Prayer for the Pilgrim Church" (see Appendix 1)

Handouts

4.1   A Catholic Teacher Reflects on the Importance of Context
4.2   Does the Bible Condemn Homosexual Activity?
4.3   What Does the Church Say About Homosexuality? (Part 1)
4.4   What Does the Church Say About Homosexuality? (Part 2)
4.5   What Does the Church Say on the Issue of LGBT Youth?
4.6   Does the Church Allow LGBT Support Groups for Young People?

Creating Safe Environments for LGBT Students
© 2007 by The Haworth Press, Inc. All rights reserved.
doi:10.1300/5723_06

Format

1. Facilitator and participants begin session with the "Prayer for the Pilgrim Church" (see Appendix 1).

2. Facilitator elicits from participants their thoughts and insights on Session 4: Reading Assignment. From both what they read and their own knowledge, what can they say about the Church's teaching on homosexuality?

3. Facilitator informs participants that the bulk of this session will be devoted to reviewing and discussing the history and development of our "pilgrim" Church's understanding and teaching on homosexuality, and the various approaches that can be employed in the Catholic high school setting in response to the issue of LGBT youth.

This exploration and discussion will be structured around four questions:

a. Does the Bible condemn homosexual activity?

b. What does the Church say about homosexuality?

c. Has the Church recommended updated information on homosexuality for teenage students?

d. Does the Church allow GLBT support groups for young people?

First though, the concept of context is introduced via Handout 4.1 "A Catholic Teacher Reflects on the Importance of Context."

In facilitating discussion about the concept of context, the following questions may be useful:

a. How does the author of this piece understand context? How do you understand context?

b. What role does context play in your day-to-day pastoral response to students?

c. What are some examples of "living with ambiguity" in your day-to-day classroom and school interactions?

d. How would you respond to a student who asks: "If I am gay, how is it that I am made in the image and likeness of God, and yet am called 'intrinsically disordered' "?

4. Facilitator elicits from participants their responses to these questions in light of what they remember being discussed in Session 1 "Laying the Foundations." After this sharing time, the facilitator presents Handout 4.2 "Does the Bible Condemn Homosexual Activity?" Participants read this handout and are encouraged to share their thoughts about its content.

5. Facilitator distributes Handout 4.3 "What Does the Church Say About Homosexuality? (Part 1)." In groups of 2-3, participants read and discuss the contents of this handout.

Suggested discussion questions:

a. Is there any information about the Church's teaching on homosexuality contained in this handout that is new?

b. Handout 4.3 suggests that Catholic educators and helping professional need to be especially mindful of three tasks. How important are these tasks to you? Why/why not? When and how could you envision engaging in these tasks?

c. In its 1986 *Letter the Bishops of the Catholic Church on the Pastoral Care of Homosexual Persons,* the Congregation for the Doctrine of the Faith states that the Church's expectation of lifelong celibacy for lesbian and gay people will "be met with bitter ridicule by some." Would you describe the perspective of Fr. Josph O'Leary as one of "bitter ridicule"? If not, how would you categorize his statements?

6. Facilitator notes that along with the various statements contained in Handout 4.3, there are other official Church teachings that collectively comprise a strong mandate to provide pastoral care for homosexual people. *It is this mandate that guides the formulation of a pastoral approach to all students within our schools.* Facilitator presents a selection of Church teachings that reflect this "pastoral mandate" (see Handout 4.4 "What Does the Church Say About Homosexuality? (Part 2)." Participants read and discuss these in light of the previous insights shared regarding the history and ongoing development of Church teaching.

7. Facilitator shares with participants Handout 4.5 "What Does the Church Say on the Issue of LGBT Youth?" and Handout 4.6 "Does the Church Allow LGBT Support Groups for Young People?" Participants share their thoughts about the implications of these handouts' content.

8. Much of the material we'll explore in this session has been recently reiterated in the United States Conference of Catholic Bishops' November 2006 document, *Ministry to Persons with a Homosexual Inclination*. Like all previous Vatican and USCCB documents, the "guidelines for pastoral care" presented in *Ministry to Persons with a Homosexual Inclination* stress that the homosexual orientation is intrinsically disordered and that homosexual acts are contrary to the natural law, incompatible with the Christian life, and always morally wrong. However, the document also emphasizes the fundamental dignity of each person as created by God.

In terms of LGBT youth, *Ministry to Persons with a Homosexual Inclination* emphasizes the necessity of friendship and community, encouragement and guidance–though stress that all such support should primarily be aimed at ensuring that young people don't get involved in homosexual relations or in the "gay subculture"–a term that the USCCB fail to define.

The USCCB's latest "pastoral guidelines" have been criticized by some Catholics for downplaying not only aspects of the 1997 USCCB document, *Always Our Children* (which many consider to be more positive and pastoral in tone), but also the place and role of one's conscience. The new document, for instance, warns those in church ministry against challenging Church teaching in any way. Many have also been critical of the bishops' failure to consult with LGBT people while drawing up the guidelines contained in *Ministry to Persons with a Homosexual Inclination.*

9. In light of these practical (and pastorally sensitive) guidelines for responding to LGBT youth, and mindful and respectful of the range of Church teaching on homosexuality, participants in groups of four to five discuss and role-play the following scenarios:

- You teach the school's Family Life course each year to seniors. Past student evaluations of this course suggest using models of family other than the nuclear family. What other types of families could be included in this course? Would you include a same-sex household as an additional model? Why or why not?
- You are a campus minister. Students have a great respect for you and many LGBT students come to you for advice and support. Due to your popularity, a small but vocal group of parents have raised concerns about you. As a result, the principal asks you to work less with LGBT students in order to "quell the controversy." How do you respond? Why?
- You come upon a male student whose locker has been defaced with homophobic graffiti. The student is quite upset and crying. You suggest accompanying the student to the office to report the incident, but the student, fearing reprisals, begs you to drop the matter completely. What do you do? Why?
- A student confides in you that he feels that he is gay. He also says that because he has never had any secrets from his parents, he has decided to come out to them. You happen to know from a separate conversation that this student's parents are extremely homophobic, and that their homophobia flows from a strict adherence to certain biblical passages and doctrinal positions. You are certain that there will be severe repercussions for the student if he comes out to them. Do you intervene? Why/why not? If you do, how do you go about it?
- As a staff person you have confidentially referred a student who is questioning her sexual orientation to the school's diversity club. The mother of this child discovers that her daughter is questioning her sexual orientation and feels very angry and distraught. The mother accuses you and the school of "crossing the line" and of "pushing the gay agenda." How do you respond to this parent?
- You catch a student defacing a bulletin board acknowledging Safe Staff initiatives being launched in your school. You confront him and he responds angrily, "Why do these fags al-

ways have to flaunt it? And why is this allowed in a Catholic school when the Bible condemns homos?" How do you respond?

10. Facilitator distributes Session 5: Reading Assignment to participants and asks that for the next session they read and reflect upon the anecdotal pieces that comprise this assignment.

HANDOUTS

Handout 4.1. A Catholic Teacher Reflects on the Importance of Context

In the pastoral care of LGBT youth, the importance of context cannot be overemphasized.

Moral instruction must at all times be given in the broader context of Catholic Social Teaching and in particular, context of the individual. That is to say, the pastoral care and response to a young LGBT person do not necessarily mean compromising the teaching of the Church on homosexuality. As teachers, we need to be sensitive to the individual student and the context of his or her interaction in order to accurately apply the moral instruction. Thus moral instruction must always be accurately applied to the context.

Contextualizing and then applying moral guidelines should not be misinterpreted as moral relativism, which says "it all just depends . . ." Contextualizing moral guidelines means truly understanding the situation, the student, the power of language, and the call of the Spirit at that particular time, and then employing the moral guideline appropriately.

Perhaps an example can more clearly illustrate these concepts. Imagine a student stops in after class and asks the teacher: "If I am gay, how is it that I am made in the image and likeness of God, and yet am considered 'intrinsically disordered'?" In this particular context, a student may not be asking for metaphysical definitions and a semantic analysis of two opposing views of the human person. Instead, the student is engaging the teacher in human contact, from one whom he or she trusts to guide him or her and to reassure him or her of their worth. It is my belief that in this context, the teacher must affirm the human life before him or her, and that simply repeating the "love the sinner, hate the sin" line is an inappropriate response to this young person.

In this instance, and in so many others, a teacher needs to develop the ability to live with ambiguity. While the moral instruction is not ambiguous, fully understanding the context and appropriately responding to a young person will be.

Handout 4.2. Does the Bible Condemn Homosexual Activity?

The following is a summary of a presentation made on March 14, 2001, by William Hunt at an event sponsored by the Catholic Pastoral Committee on Sexual Minorities.

Why does this question matter?

Today there is a consensus among Catholic Church authorities that homosexual orientation is not sinful. However, these same authorities consider homosexual activity to be wrong and cite biblical texts to support their opinion. This provides a rationale for discrimination. They argue that just as we discriminate against active alcoholics by denying them driver's licenses, so also it is reasonable to discriminate against lesbian and gay Catholics who are sexually active.

In effect, these Church authorities are saying: "Who you are is holy, but what you do is sinful. On this basis, you can be excluded from leadership positions in the Church and even from the sacraments." Consequently, it is vitally important to examine whether the Bible does, in fact, condemn every kind of homosexual activity. If it does not, then all of us, including Church authorities, need to reevaluate this discriminatory stance.

Do any of the biblical authors specifically condemn homosexual activity?

No. Homosexual orientation is a twentieth-century concept and was as unknown to the biblical authors as were organ transplants or atomic energy. They never considered the morality of affectionate genital sexual relations between consenting adults whose basic psychosexual orientation was toward persons of the same gender.

Are some forms of same-sex activity condemned by some of the biblical authors?

Yes. Israelites and their Semitic neighbors in a highly patriarchal society evaluated sexual relations between men in terms of their core values of purity, reproductivity, and especially masculine honor. To distinguish themselves from other peoples, Israelites forbade such things as cross-breeding cattle, sowing two kinds of grain in one field, wearing a garment made from two kinds of fabric, eating shrimp, and engaging in same-sex genital activity. These were all things that gentiles did. (See Leviticus: 19:19, 11:10-11.) One's social status and profession was set at birth, and a man's highest aspiration was to have male children to carry on his father's name. For them, same-sex genital activity was like sowing seed on a barren field. Finally, it offended their sense of honor for a man to be penetrated by another man because in their patriarchal culture, it reduced him to the role and status of a woman.

Does the rationale for the biblical condemnation extend to the Church in our day and age?

No. Already in the first century of the Christian era that rationale was discarded. In the wake of the successful mission to the gentiles, most—if not all—of the "purity rules" of Leviticus were abandoned. Jesus also radically undermined the value of reproductivity. He abandoned his inherited social status as a wood worker to become a wandering preacher. At odds with his own family, he instructed his followers to turn their backs on the most sacred family obligations of their patriarchal age. In the Gospels, Jesus never mentions his earthly father, appears to have been unmarried, and had no children.

Finally, Jesus radically undercut the rigid distinction between the sexes that was so much a part of a culture based on patriarchal-based honor. There were women among his disciples and friends. Jesus is portrayed in the Gospels as speaking with women in public; performing miracles on their behalf; and praising the wisdom of their responses. At the Last Supper, he even assumed the role of a woman when he washed the feet of his disciples.

Can we say, then, that the Bible approves of affectionate sexual relations between committed lesbian or gay couples?

No. All that one can say is that the biblical record does not rule out the possibility that the Church will develop a more positive evaluation of homosexual activity.

That is what appears to be going on right now as the Church takes a pastoral approach to LGBT persons. Pastoral ministry both takes its inspiration from the Scriptures and returns to those same Scriptures with new questions. These new questions engender controversy and a deeper scrutiny of the biblical witness. The process can take many centuries, but after much discussion and prayerful reflection, a new consensus emerges.

John Henry Newman liked to quote the ancient maxim: "A tranquil world is the final judge." Once the dust settles it is easier to see where the road leads. Today, with regard to the moral evaluation of homosexual activity, the world of the universal Church is anything but tranquil. Hence, the critical importance of serious intra-Church dialogue on issues raised by ministry to LGBT Catholics.

Handout 4.3. What Does the Church Say About Homosexuality? (Part 1)

Recent Official Church Teaching Regarding Homosexual Orientation and Behavior

The teaching of the Catholic Church with regard to homosexuality includes five distinct areas: homogenital behavior, homosexual orientation, pastoral ministry, prejudice against homosexual persons, and human and civil rights.

These five areas were first identified and explored by the U.S. Conference of Catholic Bishops (USCCB) in the 1976 pastoral letter, *To Live in Christ Jesus.* Subsequent USCCB documents, along with those issued by the Vatican's Congregation for the Doctrine of the Faith, attempt to further explore and explain each of the five areas of the Church's teaching on homosexuality. The most recent of these documents is the USCCB's *Ministry to Persons with Homosexual Inclinations: Guidelines for Pastoral Care* (November 2006).

1. Homogenital Behavior

According to the *Catechism of the Catholic Church,* homogenital activity is . . . "intrinsically" immoral and "objectively" wrong. Therefore, the Church expects all lesbian and gay persons to be sexually abstinent. Almost every Church document that deals with homosexuality explicitly states this part of the teaching.

The following four statements, for instance, are from the Congregation for the Doctrine of the Faith's 1986 *Letter to Bishops of the Catholic Church on the Pastoral Care of Homosexual Persons:*

> Although the particular inclination of the homosexual person is not a sin, it is a more or less strong tendency ordered toward an intrinsic moral evil; and thus the inclination itself must be seen as an objective disorder.

> To choose someone of the same sex for one's sexual activity is to annul the rich symbolism and meaning, not to mention the goals, of the Creator's sexual design. Homosexual activity is not a complementary union, able to transmit life: and so it thwarts the call to a life of that form of self-giving which the Gospel says is the essence of Christian living. This does not mean that homosexual persons are not often generous and giving of themselves; when they engage in homosexual activity they confirm within themselves a disordered sexual inclination which is essentially self-indulgent. As in every moral disorder, homosexual activity prevents one's own fulfillment and happiness by acting contrary to the creative wisdom of God.

> There is a clear consistency within the Scriptures themselves on the moral issue of homosexual behavior. The Church's doctrine regarding this issue is thus based, not on isolated phrases for facile theological argument, but on the solid foundation of a constant Biblical testimony. It is also essential to recognize that the Scriptures are not properly understood when they are interpreted in a way which contradicts the Church's living Tradition.

> What, then, are homosexual persons to do who seek to follow the Lord? Fundamentally, they are called to enact the will of God in their life by joining whatever suffering and difficulties they experience in virtue of their condition to the sacrifice of the Lord's Cross. That Cross, for the believer, is a fruitful sacrifice since from that death comes life and redemption. While any call to carry the Cross or to understand a Christian's suffering in this way

will predictably be met with bitter ridicule by some, it should be remembered that this is the way to eternal life for all who follow Christ. . . . Christians who are homosexual are called, as all of us are, to a chaste life.

Another Church statement relating to homogenital behavior is as follows:

[We] believe that it is only within a heterosexual marital relationship that genital sexual activity is morally acceptable. Only within marriage does sexual intercourse fully symbolize the Creator's dual design, as an act of covenant love, with the potential of co-creating new human life. Therefore, homosexual genital activity is considered immoral. (National Conference of Catholic Bishops, *Human Sexuality: A Catholic Perspective for Education and Lifelong Learning,* 1990)

2. Homosexual Orientation

The second area of Church teaching concerns homosexual orientation. In the mid 1980s, a number of U.S. bishops, such as Cardinal James Hickey and Cardinal Joseph Bernardin, issued statements on homosexuality in which the homosexual orientation is described as being "not morally wrong in and of itself." Similarly, some bishops, including the Massachusetts bishops in a 1984 statement, expressed the view that homosexual orientation is "morally neutral."

Perhaps in an effort to quash such "morally neutral" ways of defining homosexual orientation, the Vatican declared in 1986 that the homosexual "inclination," though "not a sin," is nevertheless a "strong tendency ordered toward an intrinsic moral evil." Accordingly, the homosexual orientation—along with such "inclinations" as cowardice and hypocrisy—is labeled by the Vatican as an "objective disorder."

Although the particular inclination of the homosexual person is not a sin, it is a more or less strong tendency ordered toward an intrinsic moral evil; and thus the inclination itself must be seen as an objective disorder. (Congregation for the Doctrine of the Faith, *Letter to Bishops of the Catholic Church on the Pastoral Care of Homosexual Persons,* 1986)

Then for the first time in a magisterial document, the letter admits the possibility that the homosexual orientation may not be the result of deliberate choice. For instance, the inclination to rash judgment is disordered, the inclination to cowardice, the inclination to hypocrisy—these are all disordered inclinations. Consequently homosexual persons are not the only ones who have disordered inclinations. (Archbishop John Quinn, 1987, commenting on the 1986 statement from the Congregation for the Doctrine of the Faith)

For many, the 1986 Letter to Bishops of the Catholic Church on the Pastoral Care of Homosexual Persons and subsequent teachings that reiterate the "objectively disordered" nature of homosexual orientation, represent a fundamental shift in Catholic theology. Many consider the idea of homosexual orientation predestining one toward evil as a violation of centuries of Catholic teaching on free will.

In 1990 the U.S. National Conference of Catholic Bishops sought to clarify the Vatican's statements:

To speak of the homosexual inclination as "objectively disordered" does not mean that the homosexual person as such is evil or bad. Furthermore, the homosexual person is not the only one who has disordered tendencies or inclinations. All human beings are subject to some disordered tendencies. (U.S. National Conference of Catholic Bishops, *Human Sexuality: A Catholic Perspective for Education and Lifelong Learning,* 1990)

Yet for many LGBT Catholics and their families and friends, such words are cold comfort in the face of what is experienced as the Vatican's increasingly homophopic rhetoric.

In its 2003 *Considerations Regarding Proposals to Give Legal Recognition to Unions Between Homosexual Persons,* for instance, the Congregation for the Doctrine of the Faith declared that Catholics who support or advocate legal recognition of homosexual unions are supporting or advocating evil. The document also declares that same-sex parents are "doing violence" to their children, though it fails to support such a claim with any empirical data.

In fact, according to a report by the American Academy of Pediatrics, (2002) the current scientific evidence demonstrates that children who grow up with one or two gay and/or lesbian parents "fare as well in emotional, cognitive, social, and sexual functioning as do children whose parents are heterosexual". "Children's optimal development," concludes the report, "seems to be influenced more by the nature of the relationships and interactions within the family unit than by the particular structural form it takes."

For many, the fact that the Vatican does not allow its teaching on homosexuality to be informed by such findings and insights is a sad and disturbing indication of intellectual dishonesty, resulting in pronouncements that are devoid of both wisdom and compassion.

Yet the ill-informed and harsh pronouncements from the Vatican regularly make the news and are thus heard by youth. If gay marriages are labeled by the pope as evil, what message does this send about gay people? And how do such messages impact our LGBT and questioning students? What effect do such statements and their implied messages have on young people's self-concept, identity formation, and spiritual development?

In light of such important questions, Catholic educators and helping professionals need to be especially mindful of the following three tasks:

1. We need to be able to confidently and competently articulate the Church's official teaching on homosexuality.
2. We need to remember and, when appropriate, articulate the reality that this teaching is not infallible. Indeed, no Catholic ethical teaching is defined infallibly. Certain beliefs have been proclaimed infallibly, but never an ethical teaching. Catholic theologian, author, and psychotherapist, Daniel Helminiak, has argued that this is because "the Catholic mind is smart enough to know that right and wrong often depend on concrete circumstances and limited human understanding" (2006). Because Catholic teaching on homosexuality is not infallible, we can reasonably say that it is therefore still in process; it is ongoing.
3. We need to be aware that a growing number of Catholic theologians, pastoral ministers, educators, parents, and individuals, consider the Vatican's current teaching on human sexuality, and on homosexuality in particular, to have denied and closed itself off to this ongoing process. As a result, many Catholics are respectfully dissenting from the Church's official teaching on human sexuality.

Catholic priest and theologian, Joseph O'Leary (1998), succinctly sums up the views of many when it comes to this dissent as it relates to the Vatican's understanding of homosexuality:

Church discourse on gay people is heavily reliant on dehumanizing objectifications, referring constantly to objectively disordered "tendencies" or "dispositions" or "inclinations" and to "objectively immoral acts." When the Vatican documents seek to give themselves an air of scientific respectability, as they tell gay people the "objective truth" about their sexual identities, they parody the jargon of old-fashioned homophobic psychoanalysts, who had never learned to listen to their 'patients' or to let them speak from their own lived experience.

In these utterances there is no respect shown to the freedom and intelligence of the addressee's moral conscience. It is taken for granted that gay people have no moral insights of their own which could enrich and correct Church tradition.

Any questioning is dismissed *a priori* as stemming from an erroneous conscience, which is seen as having no right to express itself (whatever Vatican II may have said on the matter).

The Gospel preaches an inclusive community, where the outcast has the place of honor. The tone and content of Christian teachings on gay and lesbian sexuality should build up such community, one in which human beings can share their feelings and thoughts openly, without having to wear carefully tailored masks.

To evangelize our discourse we need first to humanize it. And perhaps to humanize it would already be to evangelize it. The prophets called not for hearts of bronze but for hearts of flesh, not for sacrifice but for mercy; they had seen enough of the ravages of inhuman law.

Jesus, in turn, rooted his teachings in one value only. We wait for the Church to address to her gay and lesbian sons and daughters a message reflecting that value in both tone and content, and showing, as a kind mother should, that love is a reality, not just a verbal pawn in a game of control and condemnation.

Handout 4.4. What Does the Church Say About Homosexuality? (Part 2)

3. Pastoral Ministry

As was noted in Handout 4.1, the Catholic Church advocates sensitive pastoral care for homosexual persons.

Yet according to the Congregation for the Doctrine of Faith's 1986 *Letter to Bishops of the Catholic Church on the Pastoral Care of Homosexual Persons,* for any pastoral program to be "authentic," it must exclude any organization in which homosexual persons associate with each other that does not clearly state that homosexual activity in "immoral."

For LGBT Catholics in the United States, this was an obvious attempt to undermine Dignity, the nation's largest LGBT Catholic organization, and one which has consistently dissented from the Vatican's teaching on the "intrinsically disordered" nature of homosexuality and the sinfulness of all homosexual activity. Since Dignity's founding in 1969, many of its local chapters had been meeting on Church property. Such gatherings were widely banned, however, as a result of the Congregation for the Doctrine of the Faith's 1986 letter.

For many American Catholics, a more sensitive pastoral response to the issue of homosexuality was to be found in the U.S. Conference of Catholic Bishops' 1997 publication, *Always Our Children: A Pastoral Message to Parents of Homosexual Children and Suggestions for Pastoral Ministers.*

It seems appropriate to understand sexual orientation (heterosexual or homosexual) as a deep-seated dimension of one's personality and to recognize its relative stability in a person. A homosexual orientation produces a stronger emotional and sexual attraction toward individuals of the same sex, rather than toward those of the opposite sex. . . . Generally, homosexual is experienced as a given, not as something freely chosen. By itself, therefore, a homosexual orientation cannot be considered sinful, for morality presumes the freedom to choose.

How can you [parents of LGBT children] best express your love—itself a reflection of God's unconditional love—for your child? . . . First, don't break off contact; don't reject your child. A shocking number of homosexual youth end up on the streets because of rejection by their families. This, and other external pressures, can place young people at a greater risk for self-destructive behaviors like substance abuse and suicide. Your child may need you and the family now more than ever. He or she is still the same person. This child, who has always been God's gift to you, may now be the cause of another gift: your family becoming more honest, respectful, and supportive. Yes, your love can be tested by this reality, but it can also grow stronger through your struggle to respond lovingly.

You can help a homosexual person in two general ways. First, encourage him or her to cooperate with God's grace to live a chaste life. Second, concentrate on the person, not on the homosexual orientation itself. This implies respecting a person's freedom to choose or refuse therapy directed toward changing a homosexual orientation. Given the present state of medical and psychological knowledge, there is no guarantee that such therapy will succeed. Thus, there may be no obligation to undertake it, though some may find it helpful. All in all, it is essential to recall one basic truth. God loves every person as a unique individual. Sexual identity helps to define the unique persons we are, and one component of our sexual identity is sexual orientation. Thus, our total personhood is more encompassing than sexual orientation.

4. Prejudice Against Homosexual Persons

In 1983, some interpreted statements made by the Washington State Catholic Conference, as meaning that prejudice against lesbian and gay persons is a greater infringement of the Christian moral norm than is homosexual activity.

The Congregation for the Doctrine of the Faith sought to clarify this and other related matters in its 1986 *Letter to Bishops of the Catholic Church on the Pastoral Care of Homosexual Persons.*

> It is deplorable that homosexual persons have been and are the object of violent malice in speech or in action. Such treatment deserves condemnation from the Church's pastors wherever it occurs . . . the intrinsic dignity of each person must always be respected in word, in action and in law.

> Today, the Church provides a badly needed context for the care of the homosexual person when she refuses to consider the person as a "heterosexual" or a "homosexual" and insists that every person has a fundamental identity: the creature of God, and by grace, His child and heir to eternal life.

There was one part of the 1986 Letter, however, that many found highly objectionable, as it seemed to excuse violence toward LGBT people:

> When homosexual activity is consequently condoned, or when civil legislation is introduced to protect behavior to which no one has any conceivable right, neither the Church nor society at large should be surprised when other distorted notions and practices gain ground, and irrational and violent reactions increase.

Five years later, the U.S. Conference of Catholic Bishops noted the following:

> We call on all Christians and citizens of good will to confront their own fears about homosexuality and to curb the humor and discrimination that offend homosexual persons. We understand that having a homosexual orientation brings with it enough anxiety, pain, and issues related to self-acceptance without society adding additional prejudicial treatment. In the pastoral field, we reaffirm that homosexual men and women "must certainly be treated with understanding" and sustained in Christian hope. Their moral responsibility ought to be judged with a degree of prudence. Parents, teachers, confessors, and the whole "Christian community should offer a special degree of pastoral understanding and care," particularly since having a homosexual orientation generally precludes a person from entering marriage. (U.S. National Conference of Catholic Bishops, *Human Sexuality: A Catholic Perspective for Education and Lifelong Learning*, 1991)

Throughout the 1990s, various bishops and theologians weighed in on the issue of prejudice against homosexual persons. Cardinal Roger Mahoney, for instance, made the following remark in 1996:

What is asked of the gay community is not different from what is asked of me and anyone else. The demands of disciples of Jesus Christ are very difficult. The Church's teaching on sexuality is problematic for everyone. Racism and segregation are more flagrant violations of discipleship than sexual activity. (Cardinal Roger Mahoney, *Texas Catholic,* March 8, 1996)

5. Human and Civil Rights

In the 1991 document *Human Sexuality: A Catholic Perspective for Education and Lifelong Learning,* the U.S. National Conference of Catholic Bishops reiterated their 1976 statement that lesbian and gay persons should be accorded basic human rights. Even the Vatican in its1986 *Letter to Bishops of the Catholic Church on the Pastoral Care of Homosexual Persons*—a document that is problematic for many—noted that the intrinsic dignity of homosexual persons must be respected in law.

The intrinsic dignity of each person must always be respected in word, in action and in law. (Congregation for the Doctrine of the Faith, *Letter to Bishops of the Catholic Church on the Pastoral Care of Homosexual Persons,* 1986)

The Catholic community affirms the human dignity and worth of homosexual persons and recognizes the need for the protection of their basic human rights. Like all persons, they have a right to human respect, economic security and social equality. I remind Catholics that homosexual persons are our brothers and sisters. Prejudicial attitudes, discriminatory behavior and vicious attacks upon persons not only violate the rights of these persons, they are serious sins against the community of the Church. . . . It is the obligation of all of us to love such persons as our brothers and sisters; it is the firm intention of this local church not only to advocate for the rights of homosexual persons, but to provide competent and compassionate pastoral care for such persons. (Archbishop John Roach, *A Statement on Homosexual Persons and the Protection of Human Rights,* 1991)

It seems clear to me that gay people—like all of us—fare better when they are permitted to develop stable relationships, when they are not relegated to a same-sex society, when they are permitted to contribute their talents to relieving injustices in our society, when they are loved and respected as people striving to grow humanly and spiritually. I invite all in the Catholic community to join me in showing this kind of respect as we try work out the rightful place of these people in Church life. I ask for calm, careful study, prayer and reflection so that we can assist all members of society in the exercise of their rights, so that no one is treated as a second-class citizen or as somehow "contaminated." (Archbishop Rembert Weakland, 1980)

Handout 4.5. What Does the Church Say on the Issue of LGBT Youth?

The Second Vatican Council, in its *Declaration on Christian Education* (1965), affirmed:

> Children and young people must be helped, with the aid of the latest advances in psychology and the arts and the science of teaching, to develop harmoniously their physical, moral, and intellectual endowments, so that they may gradually acquire a mature sense of responsibility. . . . Let them be given also, as they advance in years, a positive and prudent sexual education.

The U.S. Catholic Bishops, in the *National Catechetical Directory* (1979), noted:

> Education in sexuality includes all dimensions of the topic: moral, spiritual, psychological, emotional, and physical. . . . Sexuality is an important element of the human personality, an integral part of one's overall consciousness. It is both a central aspect of one's self-understanding . . . and a crucial factor in one's relationships with others.

The U.S. Catholic Bishops, in *Education in Human Sexuality for Christians* (1981), more specifically said that teenagers

> need to understand their own sexual development . . . They need basic information regarding homosexuality. . . . They should be helped to integrate their developing sexuality into their relational lives in ways that reflect respect for themselves and others and foster mutual personal growth. . . . Knowledge, in itself, is not harmful. Therefore, every major facet of knowledge and values in relation to sexuality should be covered at some point . . . including such subjects as homosexuality. . . . To withhold knowledge or to answer questions dishonestly can only lead to misinformation and a warped set of values . . .

Other statements relating to GLBT youth are as follows:

> Educationally, homosexuality cannot and ought not to be skirted or ignored. The topic "must be faced in all objectivity by the pupil and educator when the case presents itself." First and foremost, we support modeling and teaching respect for every human person, regardless of sexual orientation. Second, a parent or teacher must also present clearly and delicately the unambiguous moral norms of the Christian tradition regarding homosexual genital activity, appropriately geared to the age level and maturity of the learner. Finally, parents and other educators must remain open to the possibility that a particular person, whether adolescent or adult, may be struggling to accept his or her own homosexual orientation. The distinction between being homosexual and doing homosexual genital actions, while not always clear and convincing, is a helpful and important one when dealing with complex issues of homosexuality, particularly in the educational and pastoral arena. (U.S. Conference of Catholic Bishops, *Human Sexuality: A Catholic Perspective for Education and Lifelong Learning,* 1990)

> When we get to the point of living our teaching authentically, no homosexual persons will have to live in fear of becoming known as they really are. Also, children who are in the process of discovering their sexual orientation will never have to be afraid of taunts and rejec-

tion for their sexual orientation, nor will they feel, "I am the only one." There will be a teacher, a priest, a religious they can turn to and look up to. They will have a model for the hope of growing up and discovering how to live a full and happy life. . . . Homosexual persons are good and loved by God. They have no reason to be in hiding. They have a right to be known, respected, and loved as they are. We are the ones who have to change our thinking. (Gumbleton, 2001)

Handout 4.6. Does the Church Allow LGBT Support Groups for Young People?

The U.S. Conference of Catholic bishops, in *Principles to Guide Confessors in Questions of Homosexuality* (1973), cautiously pointed out that lesbian and gay persons

> should seek to form stable friendships among both homosexuals and heterosexuals. On the surface, this may seem like placing the homosexual in "the proximate occasion of sin," but other elements in his/her plan of life, and spiritual direction, can temper this danger which is justified, considering his/her need for deep human relationships, and the good which will come from them in the future.

The Catholic Bishops of England and Wales, in *An Introduction to the Pastoral Care of Homosexual People* (1980), stated that the goodwill of

> Christian groups explicitly formed for the encouragement of homosexuals to cope with their difficulties must not be automatically questioned, especially because their very existence may be due to the insensitivity of the general public. . . . To condemn a social gathering simply because of possible moral dangers could lead to ridiculous restrictions. . . . This is an unhealthy attitude which destroys human relationships . . .

> Before attempting to provide spiritual guidance or counseling for a homosexual person, the pastor must be aware of his own limitations. Unconscious prejudice resulting from a biased social tradition does injustice to the homosexual and renders effective counseling impossible. No real benefit can be expected unless the pastor clears away all traces of the misunderstandings that make real communication impossible. Pastoral concern does not simply consist in the rigid and automatic application of objective norms, but must also consider the individual in the actual situation with strengths and weaknesses.

The Vatican's Congregation for Catholic Education, in *Educational Guidelines in Human Love* (1983), indicated more generally that "youth groups . . . which impinge intensely on the life of the adolescent and young adult . . . are a positive condition for formation, because the maturation of the personality is not possible without efficacious personal relationships . . ."

(To be distributed at the end of Session 4)

Catholic Youth Speak Out on LGBT Issues

At a local Catholic high school, a small but enthusiastic group of students gather on a regular basis under the guidance of one of their teachers.

"Different but the same," is a phrase you'll hear repeated often in the "Aardvark" student group and it is appropriate as the group's focus is on diversity and minority groups within their school and the wider community. As members of the group will explain: "Why Aardvark? Because who thinks of aardvarks? Who thinks of LGBT students? Students from different cultures? Or students with differing abilities? If we don't, who will? We're thinking of the aardvarks of our school—those who are different, those on the fringes but who are still part of us."

Recently, the Aardvarks directed their attention and energy to their LGBT peers by working to establish a display in their school focused on LGBT issues, such as coming out and homophobia.

The Catholic Pastoral Committee on Sexual Minorities (CPCSM) spoke with members of the group about their latest efforts at raising awareness within their school community.

CPCSM: Where did the idea come from to do a display focused on GLBT issues?

COURTNEY: I think we were just talking about different things in class one day and thought, hey, maybe we should do something on gay and lesbian people. We know a lot of people are homophobic in our school, so . . .

CPCSM: What gave you that impression?

KATE: They ran a survey through the school newspaper about what you would do if you found out your friend was gay, and, like, what your reaction would be. About 12 percent of the school said they would be homophobic.

BRAD (the advising teacher to the group): Actually, I think for that particular question about what you would do if a friend came out to you, around 40 percent answered that they would not be a friend to that person. It was pretty high.

KATE: Yeah, I didn't like that. Also in our religion class we talked about that question and we did a survey about stereotypes and people had the wrong idea about every single one.

COURTNEY: And I know that a couple of people came out in their sophomore class and I've heard a lot of people say a lot of really mean things about them.

KATE: It's not fair.

GREG: Yeah, but they just do that to, like, to try to be cool. It's a group thing. Like, if this group does this thing and you want to belong to that group, [than] you do what they want to do. It's a crowd thing.

CPCSM: Once you were aware of this homophobic element within your school, what did you decide to do to address this problem?

KATE: We wanted to make people more aware.

COURTNEY: Yeah, and one of the best ways of doing that was by using the display board.

GREG: I think that while we were having a meeting we were talking about different cultures and, like, how they've been treated badly . . . different races being treated badly. Then we moved into how gay and lesbian people are treated as badly. And from there we just wanted to make a point to people that gay and lesbian people are just different, just special, in their own way and that it's just hard for us to understand what they're going through. We just wanted to make a point.

CPCSM: Was there any reservations on anyone's part about being seen to be involved in this issue given the fact that there were such negative feelings out there toward gay and lesbian people?

KATE: Well, we all feel the same way about it. We all think it's wrong to judge somebody by it [their sexuality], just like it's wrong to judge somebody by the color of their skin or by what they believe in. So based on that it just all came together and we decided to use the most practical resource [the display board]. Everyone sees it every day.

COURTNEY: Yeah, and they may not admit that they stop and look at it for the sake of, like, being cool, but we know that everyone sees it.

GREG: There are as many negative as positive [comments]. I've talked to some kids— not about it [the display]—when all of a sudden they've brought it up. I don't know why.

CPCSM: Why is there a list of staff names on the display?

DONNA: They [are staff members who] went through some workshops and found out about, like, how to deal with it [the issue of homosexuality], how to be nonjudgmental, and how to deal with it if, like, a student came to them and told them that they were gay or lesbian . . . and [for them] not to be judgmental and say, "Oh, this is wrong and you shouldn't be like that and you'll have to make yourself different," but to help them realize that that's how some people are and to help them cope with it and not be negative.

GREG: And plus because it [the issue of homosexuality] is more known now. We notice it more than in the old days when you didn't really care about it, but now it's changing—the world's changing. It's on the TV and you see it more on the news and everything. It's just more known about now.

CPCSM: How is this issue approached in your religion classes?

COURTNEY: Mostly they take it from the point of view of how the Church teaches it. In my religion class we talked about it and, like, one girl asked that if her friend told her she was a lesbian, would it be wrong for her to not want her to spend the night at her place any more. And some people said, well, yeah it would be because just because she's lesbian she should still be your friend, while others said that their mother wouldn't let a guy over for the night even though they were just friends. And that brought up some really good conversation. We kinda just discussed different questions that people had . . . comments that people had. And we talked about what it's like from the Church's point of view—like how the Church views it [homosexuality]. And I know that the Church says that they know it's a lifelong thing, that you don't just decide, like, wake up one morning and say, "Well, I'm going to be gay today." They don't want you to get married. But we shouldn't be mean to them just because of it. And the bishop said that we shouldn't, and calls upon us not to do that . . . not to be mean to them.

CPCSM: Before you saw the list of staff who had been trained to deal with this issue and to be "safe staff," did you know that something like this was going on?

JEN: Well, kind of. We knew some teachers were being trained in this area but we weren't sure who.

CPCSM: What did you think when you first heard about this training?

COURTNEY: I thought it was cool that our teachers were getting that kind of training and learning how to deal with [the issue of gay and lesbian students].

GREG: I was just surprised because I'd never seen teachers do this before. They'd talk about genes and how we're growing up and about pregnancy before, but I'd never really heard any teachers talk about gay and lesbian people and it surprised me.

CPCSM: Was it a good surprise?

GREG: Yeah. In the schools I've been to they've talked about pregnancy, drugs, and not smoking and not drinking and driving. I'd never heard teachers talk about gay and lesbian stuff. Like when I came here and heard about this [training] that's going on, it really surprised me to hear people talking about it.

MARK: I've been in some classes with one of the openly gay kids and the teachers just treat him like normal.

COURTNEY: YEAH, I think that was one of the cool things about the training, that they know they don't have to treat him any differently. I think that's cool.

CPCSM: Do you think that for someone who is gay or lesbian, this is a supportive school overall?

COURTNEY: I think some people are pretty supportive, but I know too that some people aren't. They'll yell obscenities and stuff like that. But I know there are people you could go to who wouldn't be disrespectful.

GREG: And there are some people who are afraid to come out because they're afraid of their friends putting them down and of not being cool anymore. You know, some people want to come out but they're just afraid. But they need to come out and express what they want to say.

CPCSM: What do you think would happen if a girl wanted to bring another girl to prom? Or a boy wanted to bring another boy to prom?

COURTNEY: It would be interesting to see what our administration would do. I really don't know what would happen.

CPCSM: What would you like to see happen?

COURTNEY: I think it would be good if they let them bring who they wanted to. It would only be fair. I mean if they're going to let a guy bring a girl who he's going out with, why wouldn't they let a guy bring a guy who he's going out with?

GREG: Yeah, they have a right. Maybe some students would disagree, but others would say it's okay. So there'd probably be a very big argument among students.

JEN: I think it would be a good thing if they could bring who they want.

Michael J. Bayly
The Rainbow Spirit
Spring 1998

After reading "Catholic Youth Speak Out on LGBT Issues," reflect upon and respond to the following questions:

1. How was homophobia discovered to be a problem in the school mentioned in this article? How might the extent of homophobia be gauged in your school community?

2. What is the focus of the student group featured in this article? Does your school have an equivalent student group? Why/Why not? What would be the obstacles to the establishment of such a group?

3. What was the point the students in the article "just wanted to make?" What does this "point" imply theologically?

4. How do you think students in your school describe how the issue of homosexuality is approached in religion classes? How *would* you like students to describe how this issue is addressed?

Should Students in Catholic Schools Read LGBT Books?

An English teacher in a Catholic high school responds to concerns about the availability of literature containing LGBT characters.

Some persons have questioned the appropriateness of giving seniors in our class the choice of reading a book in which LGBT persons (real or fictional) are central to the story. I believe that reading about LGBT persons is solidly within the most orthodox teachings of the Roman Catholic Church. This belief has been shaped by a number of realities.

First, the Catholic Church clearly teaches an obligation to love our sisters and brothers who are homosexual. In 1986, for example, the Congregation for the Doctrine of Faith wrote: "It is deplorable that homosexual persons have been and are the object of violent malice in speech and action. Such treatment deserves condemnation from the Church's pastors wherever it occurs . . . the intrinsic dignity of each person must always be respected in word, in action, and in law" (1986).

In the last few years the U.S. Catholic Bishops issued a pastoral letter entitled "Always Our Children." This letter instructs us to be particularly solicitous of our gay, lesbian, bisexual, and transgender children. These young people are in special need of our care, the letter says, owing to the extraordinary challenges they face in growing up. Therefore, implicit in our mission as a Catholic school is the command to give respect, care, and love to all students—including LGBT students.

Yet before any person can love another, a certain level of understanding of that other person must be gained. One way to gain an understanding of others and their situation is to get to know their experiences and their stories by reading books, viewing videos, hearing speakers, and engaging in discussions. The assignment of reading a LGBT book is thus one small step in building a bridge of respect and understanding between homosexual people and those who do not share their sexual orientation.

It's also important to remember that reading a book does not mean that the reader approves of every action of the characters presented—be these characters real or fictitious. I think of the immorality purveyed by the works of Shakespeare, Tolstoy, Chaucer, and Hawthorne, to name just a few. We would be left with very few works of literature if all books that explore the range of people's actions—including actions that are considered "sinful"—were pulled from our schools.

In short, we read literature to gain insight and understanding, not necessarily to get moral instruction. Thus the good that can be cultivated through the reading of a book containing LGBT character outweighs any discomfort that may be encountered when reading about these same character's experiences—including those experiences that may be offensive to some.

The comments of our students tend to support this. For example, after concluding her reading of a collection of short stories about gay and lesbian teenagers titled *Am I Blue?*, a young woman stated: "I have been taught that homosexuality should be looked at with discomfort and disgust. However, reading *Am I Blue?* sparked feelings of encouragement for the characters. I recognized their feelings as true and sincere, not unnatural or inappropriate."

After reading "Should Students in Catholic Schools Read LGBT Books?", reflect upon and respond to the following questions:

1. What are the two main points that the author raises so as to justify the availability within Catholic schools of literature containing LGBT characters?

2. What are your thoughts about these points?

Parting Words . . .

The following is an edited version of a letter written to the faculty of a Catholic high school by two retiring teachers. This particular high school and the wider parish in which it was located, were not open to CPCSM's Safe Schools Initiative—largely due to the hostility of the parish priest. Copies of the letter were also delivered to the school's administration, the parish priest, and assistant parish priest. One of the authors of the letter reported that "six of the younger faculty contacted us and were very positive, expressing some shock at the information and some desire to try to do something in the future. The remainder of teachers and the pastor and his assistant made absolutely no response or reference to the letter or its contents."

On a personal note, this same author acknowledged that the Safe Schools Initiative did enable him to come out as a gay man to several of his colleagues. "[Their] positive and accepting responses made my existence at the school a bit more bearable," he said, "but did not remove the implicit hypocrisy of my continuing to be, as far as everyone else was concerned, a 'regular, married, heterosexual male.'"

This particular individual is thus left to wonder: Can closeted LGBT teachers within Catholic schools participate in safe staff training initiatives without coming out? And if they come out, are they then in danger of losing their position and/or being accused of putting their own needs before their students—or worse, of being potential "recruiters" of students to the "homosexual lifestyle"? These are questions, he notes, with no easy answers.

Fellow Faculty,

Before we leave we would like to request your individual and personal attention to a group of our students who cannot, for a variety of reasons, speak for themselves. These students make up our [school's] largest minority group and are, if not openly maligned and mistreated, so totally ignored that it is as if they do not exist at all. They are "the 10%"; our gay and lesbian students.

About four years ago, the Catholic Pastoral Committee on Sexual Minorities (CPCSM) began conducting workshops in Catholic schools . . . with the aim of creating "safe staff"— staff who would be identified to students and offer a "safe space" and a "safe support group." [Our school and one other in the archdiocese] did not participate—in our case because the pastor and administration would not allow it. We and four other staff members, however, attended several workshop sessions individually and unofficially. Since that time (due largely to some ultra conservative parents in one or two schools) the workshop groups—which included two gay alumni from our school—fell into disfavor with the Archdiocese. [Consequently], the cooperating schools have largely been frightened into retreating from their supportive positions.

This retreat, of course, does nothing to help the gay and lesbian students in our Catholic schools. It simply ignores them. It leaves them with no guidance or support from their Catholic faith; it gives them the message that "God creates you to be who you are and loves you as you are—*unless you are gay.*"

Implied in this message is the mistaken notion that homosexuality is a choice, or a "preference." In fact, no one chooses his or her sexuality, it is a part of their basic, God-given identity—a belief that even the *New Catechism of the Catholic Church* acknowledges (paragraph 2358). Homophobia—the fear and distrust of homosexuality—is almost understandable if parents think their children can easily "decide" to be gay. In fact the only choice is whether or not to *act* in ways perceived to be straight. But acting is not reality, and for a gay or lesbian it is a psychic straight jacket; a continual rejection of basic identity; an unending lie to self and others. The term "being in the closet" is thus apt. Imagine living in the dark restrictiveness of an actual closet. That is what the hiding of one's identity is like. The existence of homosexuality throughout all cultures and all times—even amidst the worst persecution and punishment—would seem to contradict the notion that sexual orientation is a deliberate choice.

The reality is these students are here and have always been here. We have come to know and speak to about a dozen gay alumni. Each one knew of three or four other students from their respective classes . . . Of those we've talked to, some have shared horror stories. One who was recognized as "queer" by his classmates was raped in the shower room by a "straight" athlete. Although this attack took place nearly twenty years ago, the victim is still suffering. Another young man who, although extremely active in school affairs and respected by teachers, reported being continually taunted at whisper level. Others reported living in fear of discovery while feeling alienated and discounted.

Bringing up the topic, of course, brings us to an institutional roadblock. Although the new *Catechism of the Catholic Church* is clear about accepting the homosexual "with respect, compassion and sensitivity" while avoiding "every sign of unjust discrimination in their regard" (paragraph 2358), this is seldom officially promulgated . . . The message of God creating us as we are also sounds a little hollow when the Catechism labels homosexuality as "a grave depravity and an intrinsic disorder" (paragraph 2357). Institutionally, the only possible message to gay and lesbian students [regarding their sexual lives] is that they are condemned by God to live a life of sexual abstinence and must regard even friendship as an occasion of sin.

We are not asking you to try and change the institution. We are asking you to continue—though hopefully more consciously and more deliberately—what you have been doing on the individual level: not allowing words such as "queer," "fag," and "dyke" in the classrooms and hallways; treating such expressions as you would racial epithets. There is no overt hostility and homophobia evident among the present faculty and that is to your credit considering the implied homophobia in our never having touched on the topic.

Since we all know that it can take as little as one positive remark from an adult to turn an adolescent's life around, surely positive references to gays and lesbians has the potential to give hope to a struggling student. The statistics regarding gay teens attempting suicide at a rate three to four times higher than that of their straight peers, and the statistics of the number of gay teens on the streets, often because they have been thrown out of their homes by their parents, are frightening. Hopefully our recent concerns for social justice and Christian community are going to include gay and lesbian students.

After reading "Parting Words . . . ," reflect upon and respond to the following questions:

1. What, according to the authors, is the theological message given to LGBT students when a school chooses to "ignore" them? How is this different from the theological implications explored in response to Question 3 of "Catholic Youth Speak Out About LGBT Issues"?

2. What is the "institutional roadblock" identified by the authors? Do you perceive what they describe as a "roadblock"? How do they hope their fellow teachers will respond to this "roadblock"? How do *you*—individually and as part of a school community—respond? How as Christians do you feel we are called to respond?

3. In the preface for this article one of the authors ponders "questions with no easy answers." Are such questions discussed by the faculty of your school? Why or why not? How might they begin to be discussed and what resolutions might such discussion engender?

Session 5

The Classroom Setting and Beyond

What is done in the actual classroom space must be consonant with and a reflection of the teacher's own inner attitude and disposition.

Genevieve Goodsil-Todd
(Catholic High School Teacher)

Topics Explored

- Establishing classrooms of respect, safety, and support.
- Ways of empowering school policy.
- Utilizing the school's "foundational stories."
- Communicating with parents.
- Establishing LGBT/Ally student groups.

Recommended Equipment/Resources

Easel with pad and markers
Masking tape
Notepads, pens, and pencils
Prayer: "A Prayer for Catholic Educators" (see Appendix 1)

Handouts

5.1 Establishing a Classroom of Respect, Safety, and Support.
5.2 Peace Zone
5.3 Sticks and Stones and Names Do Break Me
5.4 Establishing Student Groups that Support LGBT Students
5.5 Empowering School Policy
5.6 Utilizing "Foundational Stories"
5.7 Guidelines for Communicating with Parents
5.8 Guidelines for Starting a LGBT/Ally Student Group

Creating Safe Environments for LGBT Students
© 2007 by The Haworth Press, Inc. All rights reserved.
doi:10.1300/5723_07

Format

1. Facilitator begins Session 5 by sharing the prayer written by a Catholic high school teacher titled "A Prayer for Catholic Educators" (see Appendix 1).

2. Participants share experiences/insights related to Session 5 Reading Assignment.

3. Have participants read quotes from LGBT youth related to negative experiences of name-calling and feelings of alienation in the school setting.

> While I am sure that many of the faculty, including some of those in the counseling department, would have been supportive had any of us had the courage to tell our secret, there was no encouragement to believe that homosexuality was discussible. My guidance counselor, in fact, announced to our senior class, "If you guys come in here and tell me you've screwed a chick, I'll talk to you. If you tell me you're queer, I'll kick you out of my office." He will never know the long term impact of his inappropriate, unprofessional comment.

> [During my] freshmen year, a group of girls in my gym class started teasing me—saying things like, "You're such a queer. You even look a boy." As I was pulling my backpack on one day in the locker room, I was pushed to the ground by someone who was behind me. When I hit the ground, they began kicking me and screaming at me, "Dyke!" and "Faggot!"

> As a high school student in Wisconsin, I suffered through over four years of anti-gay violence. In seventh grade, after a teacher left the classroom, two boys wrestled me to the floor and acted out a rape on me, saying, "You know you want it," while the rest of the class watched and laughed. In ninth grade, two boys knocked me to the floor and urinated on me. In tenth grade, about ten boys trapped me in a hallway and kicked me in the stomach so bad that I had to go to the hospital later. It was terrible. Whenever I walked around a corner, I never knew who would be there and what they would do to me. Instead of disciplining the kids that beat me up, the school started to treat me like I was the problem. They moved me into separate classes, changed my assigned seat to the front of the bus so I had to sit with the elementary school students (even though I was sixteen), and forced me to use a separate bathroom in home economics class.

> It gets to the point where you're crying in school because the people won't leave you alone. The teachers don't do anything about it. It can drive you to the point of insanity. What they want to do is make you cry. They want to hurt you. It's horrible. I hope that the one thing people learn out of this whole thing [the Columbine High School shooting] is to stop teasing people. [Eric Harris and Dylan Klebold, the two high school shooters] couldn't take it anymore, and instead of taking it out on themselves, they took it out on other people. I took it out on myself. But it was a daily thought: "Boy, would I really like to hurt someone. Boy, would I like to see them dead."

4. Invite participants to share their current classroom and/or school rules for the prevention of name-calling What are the stated consequences of name-calling? How effective have been such rules? What have been some "success stories" relating to these rules?

5. Facilitator writes on a white board one Catholic teacher's list of "five things to consider when establishing a classroom or respect, safety, and support"—(1) the way the classroom is arranged and managed; (2) nonverbal communication; (3) language; (4) cues of inclusion; and (5) listening.

6. In small groups, participants discuss and brain-storm what these "five things" mean in a practical sense when applied to the classroom setting.

7. Participants read and discuss Handout 5.1 "Establishing a Classroom of Respect, Safety, and Support." How does this particular teacher's insights and experience compare with those of the participants?

8. Facilitator notes that an effective and simple way to manage the class and set clear guidelines for student and teacher conduct is to declare that the classroom is a Peace Zone.

The time taken at the beginning of the school year (or a course of work) to teach students about what this statement means can make a big difference in classroom atmosphere. Just as the absence of war is not peace, an apparent lack of blatant acts of prejudice does not mean that the classroom is safe for every student. Taking a proactive stance by declaring the classroom a peace zone is a do-able and practical initiative.

The Peace Zone statement can remind staff and faculty that every student (and every faculty and staff member) has the basic right to a respectful, safe, and supportive environment that fosters positive self-esteem, respect for others, and academic success. This statement can be read out loud and then discussed. It could be anchoring to ask students how this proclamation can be applied in school.

9. Participants view and discuss an example of a Peace Zone statement (Handout 5.2). Does such a statement exist in their schools? Could they envision declaring their classrooms as Peace Zones? What are some strengths of the example provided? What could be some potential problems? How might these be overcome?

10. Facilitator notes that another way of building a classroom of respect, safety, and support is by integrating issues of sexual identity into diversity education activities. Participants view, role-play, and discuss Handout 5:3. "Sticks and Stones and Names Do Break Me"—a lesson plan devised by a Catholic high school teacher for teaching respect for all.

11. Participants view and discuss Handout 5.4 "Establishing Student Groups that Support LGBT Students."

It is important to note that for several years high schools have organized various groups to meet student needs and interests. For example, students can meet regularly to discuss how their own family is in transition due to divorce. By allowing the student to meet with an adult moderator to share common thoughts and feelings, the school strives to respect and support the reality of all students and provide a safe place to do so.

Just because students are allowed to meet to discuss divorce does not mean that the school is undermining the teachings of the Church or advocating divorce. In the same way, permitting student groups that promote respect for all students or which allow students to discuss common thoughts and feelings around homosexuality, homophobia, harassment, and discrimination, does not mean that these groups are promoting homosexual behavior. Rather, in both cases the Catholic school is seeking to address the reality of students. Thus building upon the directives of *Catechism of the Catholic Church,* the descriptions contained in Handout 5.4 could be used for the formation of groups within the Catholic high schools that support LGBT youth.

In light of the suggestions offered by Handout 5.4, the facilitator notes that it is essential for a teacher to choose what he or she wants to accomplish based on his or her particular school climate at the current time. One might consider developing bigger, more long-term goals ("stretch goals"), by breaking them down into smaller pieces ("smart goals"), and accomplishing one piece at a time. SMART goals are goals that are specific, measurable, attainable, relevant, and trackable.

12. Participants read and discuss Handout 5.5 "Empowering School Policy," which addresses how one begins the process of positively influencing school policy and thus extending Safe School initiatives beyond the classroom and to the entire school community.

13. Facilitator acknowledges that in order to extend Safe School initiatives beyond the classroom and to the whole school community, it is importance to get school leadership on board, to focus on school policy, and to communicate effectively with parents.

In relation to the first of these, there are three distinct steps that one can undertake so as to encourage and inspire school leadership to embrace and embody Safe School initiatives:

- *Identify and invite three individuals from the school community:*
    —An individual who possesses relevant and/or necessary information.
    —An individual with interest in assisting with the work, either because of his or her role in the school or because of genuine interest/passion about LGBT issues.
    —An individual with influence over others or over the decision-making process.

It's important to remember that "leadership" exists not only in administration but among support staff and faculty as well. It is this network of leadership that a teacher can bring together to explore the development of Safe Staff initiatives as well as to create ownership and support for other diversity initiatives.

- *Within the school network you've established, it is now important to carefully examine the history and culture specific to your Catholic high school.*

Specifically, what is the story of the school's foundation? What, if any, religious order created the school? What is the founding story of that religious order? In short, what we're trying to determine is the fundamental story and how that story is embedded in the mission and values of the school. Obviously, every school's mission is to educate students. However, the unique charisma of a school (which flows from its sponsors) fulfills this mission in a particular way. Teachers can make a strong case for creating a Safe School program by exploring and emphasizing that such an initiative is an extension of the school's mission and values.

14. As a way of demonstrating this latter point, the facilitator shares Handout 5.6 "Utilizing Foundational Stories," which provides an example of how the foundational stories of sponsors are embedded in a particular school's mission and values. Note: the name of the school has been changed.

- *The final part of the process of getting leadership on board is to make the case that Safe Staff initiatives are simply an extension of the kind of education the school has always sought to provide.*

Examining how the foundational story is embedded in the mission and values (see earlier), and presenting it first to the president and principal, then to the entire faculty and staff, and then, eventually, to the board can be a solid first step in getting the whole school community involved.

It's important to remember, however, that depending on school culture, the order of these presentations and the process involved will need to be adapted.

15. Facilitator notes that if Catholic high school faculty and staff are led through a process of reflecting on the purpose of the school, there may be hope that those who are reluctant will at least see the logic of giving every student the opportunity to learn in an environment that is safe for him or her.

The facilitator also notes that one reason why diversity initiatives often fail is that they are oriented toward changing people's viewpoints. The assumption being as follows: if a person has a change of heart, she or he will do things differently. There are more than a few diversity consultants who state that trying to change someone's view is the least successful approach. It would be ideal if everyone who heard a few LGBT students' stories, had a change of heart, and then treated every LGBT person respectfully. In reality, this is not how it works. Ideally, one would want individuals and organizations to go through a conversion process and then make policy changes. In reality, however, some do have a change in views, but many more need the influence of policy to affect their skills.

16. Facilitator shares Handout 5.7 "Guidelines for Communicating with Parents." How do such guidelines resonate with participants? Are there others that can be added?

17. Facilitator shares the following information about the history and characteristics of Gay/Straight Alliances, along with their strengths and limitations within the Catholic high school context.

Gay/Straight Alliances were formed to promote advocacy for LGBT students in schools. These school clubs are run by and for students, with a faculty/staff moderator as required by the school's cocurricular guidelines. To date, there are over 2,000 Gay Straight Alliance (GSA) clubs registered in the United States, with the vast majority of them in public schools.

The first Gay/Straight Alliance was actually formed in an independent school in Massachusetts. In 1988, Kevin Jennings, a history teacher at Concord Academy came out to the student body during a chapel reflection. It was then that he created the first GSA in the country.

Beginning with developing support and advocacy for gay students, Jennings expanded his initiative to create a cohesive network of teachers, parents, and other members of the community. The original teacher organization was called "School's Out." By 1993, the network was renamed the Gay and Lesbian and Straight Education Network (GLSEN), and its influence was recognized nationally. Massachusetts became the first state to prohibit discrimination against public school students based on sexual orientation. It was antidiscrimination legislation, however, which did not extend to private school students. In 1995, Jennings was named GLSEN's first executive director, and today there are over ninety chapters across the United States.

With the tremendous resources available through GLSEN to Gay/Straight Alliances across the country, it is important to ask whether or not the organization can be adapted to the private school—specifically, the Catholic one. To address this question, it is important to recognize that the name "gay/straight alliance" is uniquely linked to the national organization, GLSEN. While GLSEN's primary goal is the development of safe schools for LGBT students, it also seeks to influence national educational policies. While a Catholic school can benefit from the many resources available from GLSEN, it may do so at the cost of becoming affiliated with a national organization that does not align with official Church teaching.

Even though tools and resources are plentiful from GLSEN, this organization does not comply with the guidelines provided by Church teaching. Specifically, while there is agreement concerning the obligation to respect all people, there is no adherence to the Church's teaching regarding abstinence for the homosexual. Therefore, any Catholic school that seeks to form a GSA must be willing and prepared to explain its connection, if any, to the GLSEN organization. This association, if in name only, can be problematic. It could well be that the association is too strong and it is much more important to provide support for LGBT students and their allies than to use a title that draws unnecessary concern. It may be better that a supportive organization be developed and that the students themselves provide the group its name. In one Catholic high school, the students kept the acronym GSA, but had it represent the "Growing Seeds of Alliance."

18. Participants observe and discuss Handout 5.8 "Guidelines for Starting a GLBT/Ally Student Group."

- In your English literature class you have assigned the classic gay novels *The Front Runner* by Patricia Nell Warren, and *Tales of the City* by Armistead Maupin as book reports. The chair of your department hears about the assignment and confronts you. He tells you that these books are completely inappropriate for you to assign for reading in a Catholic school and asks you to withdraw the assignment. You feel it is a matter of integrity for you to provide diverse well-written literature. What arguments do you use with the department head to present your case?

- As school counselor, you have been counseling a student about sexual identity concerns. The student's mother finds out that her child is seeing you, though is not aware of any specifics. She calls you by phone and states that as the child's parent, she has a right to know why her child has been seeking counseling from you. How do you respond to this parent's demands and the concerns that underlie them? What reasons do you give to support your stance?
- You are a member of a policy committee that recommends including sexual orientation across the board in all school policies. A minority of committee members argues that the law that dictates inclusion of "sexual orientation" in official organizational statements exempts religious affiliated schools. One of the members with a legal background even suggests that to enact such policies would encourage openly LGBT teachers to apply for jobs and might also encourage presently closeted LGBT teachers to feel they have legal redress to come out. How would you proceed with the discussion? Why?
- A student has shared with you that another student whom she knows to be gay is being harassed and physically assaulted by other students from your school on a regular basis. This abuse occurs as the student makes his way home from school. The student who is sharing this information also names some of the perpetrators. Despite the reporting student's well-meaning concerns, you have no firsthand knowledge about the victimized student's sexual orientation. What do you do? Why?
- You are a single campus minister at your Catholic high school. In your ministry, you are known as a great support to students, especially LGBT and questioning students. A rumor going around is that you yourself are homosexual and are promoting your "lifestyle" with the students. You become aware of this rumor through a meeting with the school principal. How do you feel about these perceptions? What might you do about it, or, would you do anything at all?

HANDOUTS

Handout 5.1. Establishing a Classroom of Respect, Safety, and Support

1. *The way the classroom is arranged and managed*

Students can discern a "good or bad feel" from a teacher by the way a classroom is arranged and managed. One student felt that a particular teacher did not care about the students because all of the desks were set very close together, in rows facing front, while the space in front of the room gave the teacher much space to move around. This sent a message to this student that the teacher did not care that the students were comfortable. Each teacher should arrange the classroom in a way that allows him or her to teach effectively and allows students the most comfort.

2. *Nonverbal communication*

Students have shared with me the importance of eye contact, offering a greeting when students arrive, and showing genuine interest in conversation, passing time before the class begins. Realizing that teachers have a lot going on, students still thought the simple acts of eye contact and smiling were essential.

3. *Language*

Students have also cited language as a subtle yet pervasive indicator of a teacher's awareness of respect for difference. Teachers should reflect on how ideas and lessons are explained. In her article, "Invisibility in Academe," Adrienne Rich states that when someone with the authority of a teacher names reality but does not include all aspects of reality, a fundamental disconnect occurs for the student (1994). When teachers name reality or offer lists and examples, they need to offer examples from present society, not a society where LGBT people do not exist.

4. *Cues of inclusion*

The classroom environment can contain cues of inclusion. For instance, the teacher can utilize posters, sayings, bumper stickers, objects, etc., that reveal the teacher's values of respect, safety for all students, and support for diversity. The articles chosen can be attractive and inviting of new ideas. Some may even be an extension of the school's mission and values applied specifically toward diversity. The use of the rainbow ribbon, flag, sticker, etc., may not be effective in a Catholic school setting due to the many and varied social and political associations made with it. Great care should be taken so that symbols that are selected are consistent with Church teaching.

5. *Listening*

Teachers should state their availability to listen. Listening is a sacred act and has incredible healing powers. In many instances, a student just wants to talk to a teacher because she or he is a trusted adult. Authentic listening to the heart of another is fundamental to respect, safety, and support. If a student speaks to a teacher about his or her human sexuality, the teacher needs to remember that he or she has been chosen for the sacred act of listening. The teacher should also be prepared to guide the student toward a counselor if she or he needs more professional care. Yet listening might be all that is needed.

Peace Zone

As a Roman Catholic high school,
we affirm the Body of Christ expressed in
different abilities, ages, body types, genders,
ethnic and national origins, races, religions, and sexual orientations.
Therefore all students, staff, and faculty will be
treated with dignity and respected as human beings
created in the image and likeness of God.
Prejudice, harassment, discrimination, or any form of hatred
will not be permitted here.

Handout 5.3. *Sticks and Stones and Names Do Break Me*

A strategy for teaching respect for all

Circle 1: The Indian Giver
Target Area: Race/Ethnicity

Students join hands and recite the following verse as they move in a circle:

Sticks and stones may break my bones but names will never hurt me

Students drop hands and drop to the floor. Two students remain standing in the circle.

STUDENT 1: Say, do you still have that CD player with headphones I gave you?
STUDENT 2: Yeah, it's in my locker, why?
STUDENT 1: Well, I need to get it back. Mine broke and the one I gave you is really nice.
STUDENT 2: Yeah, it's really nice but you gave it to me as a gift.
STUDENT 1: I know, I know. But I want it back. I don't have the money for a new one.
STUDENT 2: What are you? Some kind of Indian giver?

Students freeze position. Sitting students all whisper loudly: "Ouch"!

NARRATOR 1 walks to center and says:

Have you ever heard someone call someone else an "Indian giver"? Do you know where that name came from? Right now this very school and neighborhood is part of an area that once was inhabited by the Lakota Indian nation. In a treaty during the 1800s this land was "sold" to white explorers for a couple thousand dollars. To this day, this debt has not been paid. Throughout history, Native American people have tried to regain the land they once enjoyed, and they were told that they could not get back what they "sold." And yet, they did not give the land away. It was taken from them. But this truth in history is overlooked when someone is called an "Indian giver." Unlike the nursery rhyme, names can hurt. When we call someone an "Indian giver," our Native American brothers and sisters are hurt. Please stop hate speech and honor diversity.

Circle 2: What a Retard!
Target Area: Ability

Students join hands and recite the following verse as they move in a circle:

Sticks and stones may break my bones but names will never hurt me

Students drop hands and drop to the floor. One student remains standing in the circle.

STUDENT: Hey, did you guys see John in social studies today? He didn't even know where Canada was! What a retard!

Student freezes position. Sitting students all whisper loudly: "Ouch"!

NARRATOR 2 walks to center and says:

Have you ever heard someone call someone else "retarded"? Do you know where that word came from? It means a slow down and sometimes it's used to describe development of body or mind. But a lot of people use that word to put someone down, to attack them in a hurtful way. Yet every human being has ability. We are just "abled" in many different ways. Unlike the nursery rhyme, names can hurt. When we use the word "retarded" in this way, we are shaming the abilities of all of our brothers and sisters. Please stop hate speech and honor diversity.

Circle 3: The "B" Word
Target Area: Gender

Students join hands and recite the following verse as they move in a circle:

Sticks and stones may break my bones but names will never hurt me

Students drop hands and drop to the floor. Two students remain standing in the circle.

STUDENT 1: Wow Donnie, you really seem upset. What happened?
STUDENT 2: Ah, nothing.
STUDENT 1: C'mon, I don't believe you. What happened?
STUDENT 2: Mrs. Farmer told me to tuck in my shirt and that I couldn't wear my Gap sweater. I don't see the problem. The sweater is black just like the school sweatshirt.
STUDENT 1: Man, that Mrs. Farmer is such a bitch.

Students freeze position. Sitting students all whisper loudly: "Ouch"!

NARRATOR 3 walks to center and says:

So often the "b" word is used to but down people, especially women. Unlike the nursery rhyme, names can hurt. By referring to any woman as a "bitch," one is showing women disrespect, minimizing their strength, and undermining their credibility to lead. Please stop using this word. Please stop hate speech and honor diversity.

Circle 4: Just Look at How Fat She Is!
Target Area: Body Types

Students join hands and recite the following verse as they move in a circle:

Sticks and stones may break my bones but names will never hurt me

Students drop hands and drop to the floor. One student remains standing in the circle.

STUDENT: Wow, did you see how much food Kylie put on her tray today? I can't believe she eats so much—you'd think she'd care how she looks. In fact, I would say her backside is like the flu—it just keeps spreading and spreading and spreading. Just look how fat she is!

Student freezes position. Sitting students all whisper loudly: "Ouch"!

NARRATOR 4 walks to center and says:

How many of you have never been concerned about how little or much you weigh? Most of us do not like what we weigh, or, are unhappy about some part of our bodies. Our culture has taught us to see beauty in only one particular size and shape. Our culture has lied to us. Each of us has beauty in our own right and dignity. Respect does not depend on the size or type of body one has. Unlike the nursery rhyme, names can hurt. By being negative and critical of your own or someone else's weight, you are upholding an untruth of society that makes us all unhappy. Please accept the beauty of all types of people. Please stop hate speech and honor diversity.

Circle 5: That's So Gay!
Target Area: GLBT People

Students join hands and recite the following verse as they move in a circle:

Sticks and stones may break my bones but names will never hurt me

Students drop hands and drop to the floor. One student remains standing in the circle.

STUDENT: Chad wanted to wear this funny kinda green shirt that his girlfriend gave him. Dude, I said, that's so gay!

Student freezes position. Sitting students all whisper loudly: "Ouch"!

NARRATOR 5 walks to center and says:

To say "that's so gay" means to say something is stupid. This phrase, along with other names and phrases just explored, is often heard in our school. Do you know the origin of the word "faggot"? As far back as the fourteenth century, the word "faggot" referred to the bundle of sticks and twigs used as kindling for burning homosexuals at the stake—much as they burned Christians in early times. Many people today believe that the use of the word "faggot" as a negative reference to a gay man began with this medieval practice of executing gay men by burning.

NARRATOR 6: What we have been trying to show today is that language matters. What we say reflects what we think. What we think and say can affect how we act. In the United States, every citizen has the right to love or hate, but no one has the right to hurt someone else—either by word or action. Unlike the nursery rhyme, names hurt people. They can hurt Native Americans, the differently abled, women, people of all sizes, and gay, lesbian, bisexual, and transgendered people.

NARRATOR 7: Please believe in the power of your words. Please believe in the power of your self. Together, we all make a difference. Let's make not only our classroom, but also the hallways, fields, courts, and locker rooms a welcoming and respectful place for everyone. Together, let's stop hate speech and honor diversity.

Handout 5.4. Establishing Student Groups That Support LGBT Students (and Educate Faculty and Other Students)

Building upon the directives of the *Catechism of the Catholic Church*, the following descriptions could be used for the formation of groups within the Catholic high school that support GLBT youth:

GSA (Gay, Straight Alliance)

The Gay, Straight Alliance (GSA) has been organized by and for students of [name of school]. Supporting the directives of the *Catechism of the Catholic Church*, the purpose of the GSA is to educate in order to address unjust discrimination and fear, and to ensure acceptance based on respect, compassion, and sensitivity to all students, especially those with a homosexual orientation. (*Catechism of the Catholic Church*, paragraph 2358).

GLOBE (Gay, Lesbian, or Bisexual, etc.)

GLOBE is a student group that discusses issues concerning sexual identity, spirituality, culture, and the Church. Emphasizing that all are called to chastity, members meet for mutual support and friendship (*Catechism of the Catholic Church*, paragraph 2359).

A teacher may also choose to select books (for his or her classroom and/or the school library) that help Catholic students gain an understanding of gay and lesbian people.

Remember, whatever you do to build environments of respect, safety, and support, keep your goals SMART, that is, specific, measurable, attainable, relevant, and trackable.

Handout 5.5. Empowering School Policy

How does one begin the process of positively influencing school policy and thus extending Safe School initiatives beyond the classroom and to the entire school community?

1. Be clear that any Safe School initiative is aligned with the purpose of the school.
2. Look toward and place influence on school policy. Specifically, identify how the school deals with issues of difference.

Why an Emphasis on School Policy?

Likely there will be some who will always be reluctant about Safe School initiatives, but if it is stated that it is part of the policy of the school, then they must either accept such initiatives as part of their work environment, or seek work elsewhere.

For example, a teacher who once thought nothing of using a gay joke to get the attention of the class must be told that jokes of that nature are not appropriate and cannot be told again without significant consequence. Note in this example that the teacher is not being asked to change what she or he thinks is funny. Rather, she or he is being told directly that jokes about gay people cannot be used in this environment.

In short, school policies can affect the skills of those who do not necessarily have a change of heart or increased empathy for LGBT persons.

Handout 5.6. Utilizing "Foundational Stories"

Following is an example of how the fundamental, or foundational stories of the Sisters of St. Joseph of Carondelet and the Brothers of the Christian Schools, embedded in the mission and values of St. Sebastian Catholic High School, (fictitious) can be utilized to support the establishment of Safe School initiatives.

This example is based on the actual utilization of these particular foundational stories within a Catholic high school. It was a process that revealed how those who have been traditionally marginalized have held a special place in the work of service and education in the history of the two cosponsoring religious communities of St. Sebastian Catholic High School. What also came to light for the school community was the recognition that a renewed commitment to its mission and values necessarily leads to the reexamination of past approaches to diversity and how they might be redefined.

Identifying the Foundational Stories of St. Sebastian Catholic High School

Embedded in the mission and values of St. Sebastian Catholic High School are the foundational stories of its cosponsors, the Sisters of St. Joseph of Carondelet and the Brothers of the Christian Schools. The founders of both congregations heard the good news of Jesus Christ and strove to live by his inspiration and example within their particular, historical context, that is, seventeenth-century France. Thus, from their beginnings, the Sisters "have been dedicated to the exercise of 'all of the spiritual and corporeal works of mercy of which a woman is capable and which will most benefit the . . . dear neighbor': ministry to orphans, to sick poor, young girls, the destitute, and others in need" (Constitution, Sisters of Saint Joseph of Carondelet, #21).

For the Brothers, their purpose has been "to give a human and Christian education to the young, especially the poor" (The Rule of the Brothers of the Christian Schools, Part 1, chapter 1). Consequently in his particular historical context, Saint John Baptist de La Salle "gave new meaning to the school by making it accessible to the poor and offering it to all as a sign of the Kingdom and as a means of salvation" (*The Rule of the Brothers of the Christian Schools,* Part I, chapters 1-2).

As Jesus Christ came to serve those who were "traditionally marginalized," so too the fundamental story of the cosponsoring communities has been to provide services and education to those in society with little to no access to basic resources. Furthermore, they understood their mission to be part of a movement that was both immediately helpful and deeply prophetic: they addressed a need and by doing so, were an example to others of a future possibility not yet seen. Through direct service and education, they were and are, creating a more just world where resources and education are not simply available to those with access, but to everyone.

How these Foundational Stories Are Reflected in the Mission and Values of St. Sebastian's Catholic High School

St. Sebastian Catholic High School is the heir to these two extraordinary communities—the fundamental stories of which are embedded in its mission and values:

> St. Sebastian is a Catholic high school co-sponsored by the Brothers of the Christian Schools and the Sisters of Saint Joseph of Carondelet. It is dedicated to the Catholic faith and to teaching youth—especially those with limited access to educational opportunities.

St. Sebastian Catholic High School seeks to educate young men and women for opportunities in post-secondary education and to positively impact and change our world.

Not only is the mission of the school to educate young people, but it also recognizes that each young person it serves has diverse ability, culture, and background. Another way to interpret this passage is to say that as part of the school's mission, it gives preferential treatment to those whose abilities, culture, and socioeconomic background keep them apart from the traditionally dominant culture.

Developing from this mission, St. Sebastian Catholic School also emphasizes and describes the values of Catholic, Academic, Leadership, Community, Service, Diversity, and Equality.

Reviewing each description, the values of community, diversity, and equality make more explicit references to (aspects of) diversity:

Community: a body of diverse and interrelated individuals who support, care, and respect each other and seek to demonstrate these values in society.

Equality: a conscious focus on and a shared responsibility for the development of a gender fair environment.

Diversity: a conscious focus on and shared responsibility to understand and respect the differences in abilities, religions, cultures, and socioeconomic backgrounds of the school community and society.

In summary, St. Sebastian Catholic High School's mission and values explicitly recognize differences among persons. It flows from and is consonant with the fundamental stories/purpose of the Sisters of Saint Joseph of Carondelet and the Brothers of the Christian Schools. Thus it is fitting to constantly strive toward fulfilling this mission and demonstrating these values in the school's concrete operations. Doing so is not simply following the directives of a statement, but rather keeping with the institution's faith tradition.

Handout 5.7. Guidelines for Communicating with Parents About Safe School Initiatives

1. Information about Safe Staff initiatives should be given to parents with all of the other information about the school.

2. Church teaching about respect and support for LGBT persons needs to be emphasized as parents will need to be assured that the program follows the teaching of the Church on homosexuality.

3. As with getting leadership on board, communications should state that any Safe School initiative undertaken is part of the school's mission and values. (*Note:* Even when such directives are followed, there will be some who will believe that the Safe Staff initiative is a promotion of the "gay lifestyle" or the "homosexual agenda." Thus it is vital to create a support system of parents who believe in and are grateful for the presence of Safe School initiatives in their children's school.)

4. Create a fact sheet about the program that can be given to administration to assist them in responding to parents' questions or concerns. Decide ahead of time the administrator who will take these calls. It is not always helpful to forward all the calls to the teacher who is the moderator of the Safe School initiatives.

Handout 5.8. Guidelines for Starting a LGBT/Ally Student Group

A Catholic teacher offers helpful guidelines for establishing a LGBT/Ally group by drawing on insights from one such group in a Catholic high school.

1. When organizing a student group, it is important that the initiative be as student-generated and student-led as possible.

2. It is also important to remember that a group can be three people!

3. Getting started might be as simple as creating a discussion group on topics of diversity and setting the atmosphere for respect and inclusion for all students.

4. A student group/club that focuses on discussion of homophobia and respect for all students of each sexual orientation must begin with student interest. Yet generating student interest will likely come from a broader discussion and/or treatment of the school environment and diversity in general rather than from a direct reference to a "group of gay kids."

5. Depending on the school's culture, a very direct call for a sexual orientation group will not get a huge response. In fact, it may be less threatening to develop a group for students who wish to be allies for those who are LGBT. In this context, student members may know, love, and respect people who are LGBT (e.g., family members, friends, neighbors, etc.) and wish to consider ways to make the world a better place in their regard.

6. It is important to make the distinction between a student group/club and a group that may be offered and led by a therapist/counselor within the school's counseling department. Although there certainly are times when a student who is LGBT/ally may need counseling/group support, that is not the purpose of the student group/club.

7. One student group currently operating in a Catholic high school is known as Growing Seeds of Alliance. Meeting once a week during lunch, Growing Seeds of Alliance is not about discussing or promoting the "gay life style," but about educating the school community in an effort to encourage respect for, and to eliminate both overt and covert acts of discrimination against, people who might be, or might be perceived to be, homosexual.

8. The only requirement for being a member of Growing Seeds of Alliance is a concern and respect for people who are LGBT, and a willingness to be an agent of respect both in and outside of the school community.

9. Fulfilling this purpose, the Roman Catholic Church's teaching on homosexuality is not compromised or left unclear. This teaching is upheld with needed emphasis on the teaching's encouragement to address unjust discrimination and fear (*Catechism of the Catholic Church*, #2359).

10. The Growing Seeds of Alliance student group exists in large part, to address a specific problem. This problem is likely in every school and workplace, and maybe in every home. The problem is not homosexual activity among teenagers or an eroding compromise of the teaching of the Roman Catholic Church on homosexuality. Rather, the problem is fear. And fear is a consuming emotion—a sibling in the family of emotions that wants every portion and place at the table. Fear drives out both gratitude and appreciation. When someone fears someone or something, she or he cannot be grateful for or appreciate what the other brings. For example, equity is nearly impossible when a man fears a woman's increased access to decision making and power. Nothing did more to the campaign of demonizing the black man than the fear produced against him by the white male. Therefore, as long as both homosexual and heterosexual persons fear homosexuality, there is a need for a group like Growing Seeds of Alliance.

Appendix 1

Prayers and Reflections

DOES IT MATTER?

My father asked me if I am gay.
I asked, Does it matter?
He said, No, not really.
I said Yes.
He said, Get out of my life.
I guess it mattered.

My boss asked me if I am gay.
I asked, Does it matter?
He said, No, not really.
I told him Yes.
He said, You're fired, faggot.
I guess it mattered.

A friend asked if I am gay.
I said, Does it matter?
He said, Not really.
I told him Yes.
He said, Don't call me your friend.
I guess it mattered.

My lover asked me, Do you love me?
I asked, Does it matter?
He said Yes.
I told him I love you.
He said, Let me hold you in my arms.
For the first time in my life
something matters.

My God asked me.
Do you love yourself?
I said, Does it matter?
He said Yes.
I said, How can I love myself? I am gay.
He said, That is the way I made you.
Nothing again will ever matter.

Anonymous Gay Youth

Taken from *In Piecing Together a Caring Community: A Resource Book on Dismantling Homophobia* by Ann Shortall (Newfoundland-Labrador Human Rights Association).

Creating Safe Environments for LGBT Students
© 2007 by The Haworth Press, Inc. All rights reserved.
doi:10.1300/5723_08

OUR CHILDREN AND STUDENTS AS GIFTS

Bless us, O God, as we gather together,
poised to recognize and proclaim
our children and students as gifts to their society.
As parents we love them as you love us–
less perfectly, but passionately.
As teachers we educate, and hopefully equip them
 to be contributors to, and consciences of their society and their schools;
to be young people empowered by self-confidence,
self-acceptance, self-control, and self-love.

Let us celebrate their dazzling beauty–
in all of their colors, their personalities and their identities.
Let us not allow politics, points of view, or platforms
to separate us from one another, or from our children.

Let our schools be secure places–but more than secure.
Let them be dynamic, egalitarian places where the identities
and contributions of all students are valued;
where justice prevails in the halls and in the hearts of our students;
where diversity is treasured, respected and celebrated.

Enlighten us, O God, and bless us with understanding
and love for all of our children.

Amen

Mary Lynn Murphy,
mother of a gay Catholic high school alum

THE LIGHT WITHIN

There is a Light within me, deep at my core.
In relating to others, it lights my way.
A part of me, holy, this Light deep within.

As a child I celebrated the Light–as a child does,
trustingly, spontaneously, without shame.
Too soon I realized that my Light was different.
They had names for the Light I possessed,
they who did not possess it.
Like great dark clouds these names
gathered around me.
They clung to me.

In time I myself began to fear the Light,
began to perceive it as something
destructive and distorted.
The years passed.
I had not the words nor the courage
to hold forth my Light.
I feared what it would reveal about myself,
about my life.

I built a wall, a facade.
The flow of my energies was fragmented.
I turned inwards and declared my Light darkness.
For years one can slumber
but the Light remains.

A boy of fourteen, plagued by fear and doubt.
At night I roamed the darkened house,
the silent garden–lost.
A stranger in the midst of family and friends.

Alone but for the fear
which like a wild beast, a coiling serpent within,
dragged me deeper into darkness.

Each night I would pray to the God
of the psalmist who likewise had prayed:

. . . troubles surround me;
my sins have overtaken me;
I cannot see my way.
They outnumber the hairs of my head,
and my heart fails me.

Be pleased Yahweh to rescue me.
Yahweh, come quickly and help me!

. . . Poor and needy as I am,
God has me in mind.
You my helper, my savior,
my God, do not delay.

And then came the calm.
It was a gift from both beyond and within.
It rose like a tide and quelled the fiery beast of fear
and allowed me to walk upon the sacred ground
of my own true Self.

Here I cultivated a garden, a resting place,
wherein I drew strength.
And the calm became as a splashing fountain
that resounded my name.

In time I came to look upon the Light
that I had so greatly feared,
to approach its flame.
And to perceive the source of both
the calm and the Light,
the fountain and the flame,
as being one and the same.

I waited, I waited for Yahweh.
Then he stooped to me
and heard my cry for help.

He pulled me up from the seething chasm,
from the mud of the mire.
He set my feet on rock,
and made my footsteps firm.

Michael Bayly

A PRAYER FOR THE PILGRIM CHURCH

Loving God,

We give thanks for this opportunity to gather together in this place made holy by your presence within and among us.

We give thanks for the fullness of truth continually being revealed to us in new ways as we seek to discern your sanctifying presence within the diversity of our lives and our world.

We give thanks for this unfolding truth in our lives and pray that we may never boast to possess it, here and now, in its entirety least we trample upon its quiet yet insistent emergence in the lives and relationships of those whom we had previously overlooked or even shunned.

We pray that you grant us the strength to walk humbly and lovingly together as we discern your presence within the vast arena of human experience.

Gently remind us, lover God, that at our core we are a pilgrim Church, a community of spiritual seekers.

Protect us from our own hubris and from hurting ourselves and others by our insistence that we have all the answers, that we have somehow captured your boundless reality in our limited words and doctrinal statements.

Remind us again, beloved one, that we are called to be seekers—seekers focused less on possessing the truth than by being possessed by the truth as we seek to recognize and embody justice, humility, and love.

Yes, we are seekers of the transforming presence of the sacred, which as our brother Jesus lived and taught, is already deep within us and among us.

We will seek this presence in a spirit of trustful anticipation and loving respect for one another.

Be with us, loving God, not only in this journey we undertake today but in all the searching journeys we undertake as your pilgrim Church.

Amen.

Michael Bayly

A Prayer for Catholic Educators

Loving and faithful God,
You have called us to teach young people
And to be grateful stewards of Your creation.
Help us remember that every child,
Every child that enters our classroom,
Is on a sacred journey back to You.
Empower us to do all things within our capacity
To help them on their journey home.

Grant us Your grace to embody Your reign on earth;
In the way we teach, in the sacred spaces we create,
And in the policies we design and implement.

We ask this through our brother and teacher Jesus Christ.

Amen.

Michael Bayly

Appendix 2

Countering Common Fallacies and Stereotypes
of LGBT Persons

- *LGBT persons represent a negligible number of people.*

    The Kinsey study (1947) estimated that 13 percent of males and 7 percent of females are exclusively gay or lesbian (Kinsey, 1948, 1953). Judd Marmor, Professor of Psychiatry at USG Medical School has calculated that one in every four families has a member (parent or child) who is lesbian or gay (Ryan and Futterman, 1998). It is generally accepted that homosexuality, like heterosexuality, is a natural and normal variant in human sexuality and has existed in every culture and throughout history.

- *LGBT persons choose to be who they are.*

    Research indicates that sexual orientation is determined either before birth or very early in life, and that while sexual behavior can be altered, sexual orientation cannot. In a study of 161 gay men with twin or adoptive brothers, 52 percent of the subjects' identical twin brothers, 22 percent of their fraternal twin brothers, and 11 percent of their adoptive brothers were homosexual, a finding that supports the theory of a biological link (Bailey and Pillard, 1991). A study of lesbian twin sisters found similar results: the identical twins of lesbians were three times as likely to be lesbian or bisexual than fraternal twins (Bailey and Pillard, 1993). Also, in a study comparing brain tissue of 19 gay men and 16 heterosexual men, there was a significant size difference between the two groups in a cluster of cells in the hypothalamus (the region involved in sexual response) (LeVay, 1991). Finally, in a study of 979 gay men and 477 heterosexual men, most said that their sexual orientation was established before adolescence, regardless of whether they had been sexually active at that time. The "decision" that is most often involved is not whether one is going to be lesbian or gay, but rather whether one is going to acknowledge the existence of gay or lesbian feelings and behaviors.

- *Most child molesters are LGBT persons.*

    Sexual abuse of children occurs primarily within the family. Most sexual abuse of children outside the family is committed by pedophiles (i.e., people who engage sexually with children). Adult lesbians and gay men are no more likely to be pedophiles than heterosexuals (Groth, 1979). Same-sex pedophilia is not an indicator of adult homosexual orientation. Several studies reveal that 90-98 percent of pedophiles and child abusers are heterosexual men (Benton County Sheriff's Office).

- *You can always tell by how they look, dress, or act.*

    The vast majority of lesbians and gay men cannot be identified by their physical appearance. The small fraction who dress or act so that people will assume they are gay usually do so because they want to be known as gay or lesbian or because they dislike the traditional gender roles. Many straight people appear lesbian or gay for this reason too. But if most people are aware only of those

Creating Safe Environments for LGBT Students
© 2007 by The Haworth Press, Inc. All rights reserved.
doi:10.1300/5723_09

lesbians and gay men who fit the stereotypes, and if the media plays up the stereotypes, it's logical that people will believe the stereotypes.

- *Homosexuality is a type of mental illness that can be cured by appropriate psychotherapy.*

In 1973 the American Psychiatric Association removed homosexuality from its list of mental disorders (it had been listed as a sociopathic personality disorder). Two years later, the American Psychological Association (1975) publicly supported this move, stating that "homosexuality per se implies no impairment in judgment, reliability or general social and vocational capabilities . . . (and mental health professionals should) take the lead in removing the stigma of mental illness long associated with homosexual orientation." Furthermore, research done by the National Institute of Mental Health found no greater incidence of mental illness among lesbians and gay men than among heterosexuals.

In 1990 the American Psychological Association stated that scientific evidence does not show that reparative or conversion therapy works and that it can do more harm than good. Changing one's sexual orientation is not simply a matter of changing one's sexual behavior.

- *LGBT persons' lifestyles are contrary to family values as LGBT people are obsessed with sex and lead promiscuous lives.*

The so-called homosexual lifestyle involves the same things as the "heterosexual lifestyle"—family, home life, career, feelings and actions of love, commitment and sexual expression, grocery shopping, movie-watching, political activism, and so on. While it is true that some LGBT people engage in self-centered and dangerous behavior, the same is true of some straight people. Yet since the "straight lifestyle" is not defined by this type of behavior, why then should the LGBT lifestyle? Furthermore, it is misleading to lump all LGBT people or all straight people into one of two "lifestyles." The reality is that there are as many lifestyles as there are people—gay or straight.

- *Homosexuality is caused by bad parenting.*

There is no evidence, according to the Kinsey Institute, that male homosexuality is caused by dominant mothers and/or weak fathers, or that female homosexuality is caused by girls having exclusively male role models. Furthermore, studies of children raised by homosexual and by heterosexual parents reveal no developmental differences between the two groups in the areas of intelligence, psychological adjustment, social adjustment, development of social sex role identity, or development of sexual orientation.

- *Homosexuality is caused by negative experiences with the opposite sex. All they need is to have some positive experiences with a member of the opposite sex.*

There are no "cures." Many lesbians and gay men have had satisfying heterosexual experiences in their lifetime. However, gay men and lesbians who, out of desperation or fear, choose to enter a heterosexual relationship to get "cured" may cause undue misery and pain to themselves, their partners, and any children that may result from such a relationship. Most gay men and lesbians would not choose to be sexually active with members of the opposite sex and would resent and challenge the assumption that heterosexuals have a "corner on the market" of satisfying sexual relationships.

- *There are no "bisexuals." Most people are either completely homosexually or heterosexually oriented.*

The pioneering studies of Dr. Alfred Kinsey and his associates are most frequently cited on this question. This data suggested that, in fact, few people are either predominately heterosexual or homosexual. Most people fall somewhere on the continuum between these two ends of the scale and, thus, have the capacity to experience both affectional and sexual feelings for members of both sexes. Those who fall in the middle are thus capable of being attracted to both the same and the opposite sex.

- *The gay agenda is antifamily and is trying to destroy the institution of marriage and the family.*

   By using the term "gay agenda" those fearful of the diversity of human sexuality are inferring that LGBT people are obsessed with sex, lead promiscuous lives, and are intent on instilling such a way of existence on all members of society. Yet when one acknowledges the diversity of LGBT lives and aspirations, the idea that a menacing monolithic LGBT group and agenda is orchestrating and advocating the overthrow of civilization as we know it becomes the ludicrous notion that it is.

   Furthermore, only 26 percent of all American households are traditional nuclear families—a figure that represents a 14 percent decrease from 1970. Half of all recent marriages are expected to end in divorce, and the number of families without an adult male parent has increased by 139 percent since 1970. Clearly, the traditional nuclear family is in decline, but it's not one brought about by LGBT people (U.S. Census Bureau, 1991).

   Recently, at both the state and federal level, efforts have been undertaken to pass a constitutional amendment that would ban civil marriages between same-sex couples. In the view of many, such an amendment would single out and demean LGBT people on the basis of their sexual orientation—one that comprises an indelible aspect of their God-given identity. This type of singling out and demeaning undermines the charity to which we are called as members of the Body of Christ. Furthermore, such an amendment would, for the first time, enshrine discrimination into the U.S. constitution. Ultimately, it would weaken families by promoting misunderstanding, fear, and bigotry.

   In Minnesota, the Catholic Pastoral Committee on Sexual Minorities (CPCSM) has been a leading Catholic voice in opposing a constitutional amendment that would ban civil marriage between same-sex couples. In a 2003 statement, CPCSM called upon Both our federal and state governments to reject such [an amendment] and to choose instead to take proactive steps so as to strengthen marriages and families in truly positive and charitable ways. Such ways include expanding prenatal and postnatal care, increasing the minimum wage to a living wage, mandating equitable family leave policies, and extending full civil protection to all families that are defined by two adult lifetime partners whose relationship is long-term and characterized by a loving and respectful emotional and financial commitment and interdependence (CPCSM, 2003),

- *LGBT persons are by nature disordered and sinners. If God really loved them, He would never have allowed them to have such an affliction.*

   This notion reflects a truly dysfunctional and unhealthy theology. First, it refuses to acknowledge the rich diversity of human sexuality as a gift from God. Second, it assumes that negative experiences are directly caused by God. Thus God is viewed as a puppet-master whom we fear, rather than a loving and ultimately mysterious reality with whom we are invited to be in relationship.

- *The Bible condemns homosexuality.*

   No biblical writer specifically condemns homosexual orientation. Homosexual orientation is a twentieth-century concept. It was as unknown to the biblical authors as organ transplants, electricity, or the role that the female plays in procreation. They never considered the morality of loving sexual relations between consenting adults whose basic psychosexual orientation was toward people of the same gender.

   The biblical writers do, however, condemn some forms of same-sex activity—a condemnation that modern biblical scholars contend stemmed from the fact that the Israelites and their Semitic neighbors lived in a highly patriarchal society. They evaluated sexual relations between men in terms of their core values of purity, reproductivity, and especially masculine honor. In such a society, a man's highest aspiration was to have male children to carry on his father's name. For them, same-sex genital activity was like sowing seed on a barren field. It also offended their sense of honor for a man to be penetrated by another man because it reduced him to the perceived lower role and status of a woman. It has also been convincingly argued that the biblical writers, in condemning some forms of same-sex activity, are actually condemning abusive power dynamics—homosexual rape, male prostitution, and sex with youth—dynamics that rightly should be challenged and denounced.

Despite this, we cannot say that the Bible approves of respectful and loving sexual relations between committed lesbian or gay couples. All that one can say is that the biblical record does not rule out the possibility that the Church will develop a more positive evaluation of homosexual activity. That is what appears to be going on right now as the Church takes a pastoral approach to LGBT persons. Pastoral ministry both takes its inspiration from the Scriptures and returns to those same Scriptures with new questions. These new questions engender controversy and a deeper scrutiny of the biblical witness. The process can take and has taken—with regard to other issues—centuries. But after much discussion, prayer, and reflection a new consensus with regard to complex human realities can and has emerged.

• *Most LGBT persons act like pagans and show hatred toward God and organized religion.*

Many LGBT have been alienated and emotionally scared by things that organized religions have said and done. These individuals often display mistrust toward an image of God and a model of Church that has belittled, ignored, or condemned their experiences. Accordingly, many LGBT people have found solace and acceptance in faith communities that are less hierarchically structured; communities that emphasize spirituality rather than religion; God within rather than God outside and removed from oneself and one's experiences. For many situated within the rigid parameters of organized religion, such spirituality-based communities may indeed appear "pagan." Yet if one of the hallmarks of any truly spiritual/religious community and/or experience is that it facilitates positive human, and by extension, societal transformation, then many LGBT people do in fact live profound spiritual/religious lives.

Appendix 3

Annotated Bibliography

THE LGBT REALITY AND CATHOLIC SCHOOLS

- Maher Jr., Michael. *Being Gay and Lesbian in a Catholic High School: Beyond the Uniform.* Binghamton, NY: The Haworth Press, 2001.

Informatively explores the problem of homophobia in Catholic education through personal testimonies of gay and lesbian former Catholic high school students and an insightful analysis of the discrepancies between current attitudes and actions and the Catholic Church's official teaching. The book also provides an extensive summary of official Catholic teaching on homosexuality and information on the psychology of gay teenagers.

BOOKS FOR PROFESSIONALS WORKING WITH LGBT YOUTH

- Jennings, Kevin (Ed.). *Becoming Visible: A Reader in Gay and Lesbian History for High School and College Students.* Los Angeles: Alyson Publications, 1994.

Drawing from both primary and secondary sources, *Becoming Visible* traces the presence of homosexuality through 2,000 years of history and a diverse range of cultures. Illustrated with excerpts and personal accounts, each section of this reader is followed by questions that teachers could assign to students as well as suggestions for classroom activities. The readings are suitable for age levels from ninth grade through college, but general readers seeking insight into gay and lesbian history will be equally enriched.

- Ryan, Caitlin and Futterman, Donna. *Lesbian and Gay Youth: Care and Counseling.* New York: Columbia University, 1998.

Reputedly the first hands-on guide for providing health and mental health care to lesbian and gay youth. Named 1998 Book of the Year in Psychiatric Nursing by the *American Journal of Nursing.*

- Schneider, Margaret S. (Ed.). *Pride and Prejudice: Working With Lesbian, Gay and Bisexual Youth.* Toronto: Central Toronto Youth Services, 1997.

Offers strategies and resources for professionals working with lesbian, gay, and bisexual youth, including a multifaceted approach to reduce risk factors for lesbian, gay, and bisexual youth, guides for counseling gay male youth, insights into the complexities of bisexual youth identities, and strategies for working with homeless lesbian and gay youth. This book can be ordered from Central Toronto Youth Services, 65 Wellesley St. E., Suite 300, Toronto, Ontario, M4Y 1G7.

Creating Safe Environments for LGBT Students
© 2007 by The Haworth Press, Inc. All rights reserved.
doi:10.1300/5723_10

- Walling, Donovan R. (Ed). *Open Lives, Safe Schools: Addressing Gay and Lesbian Issues in Education.* Bloomington: Phi Delta Kappa Educational Foundation, 1996.

  A diverse collection of essays that collectively argue that safe schools are schools where it is safe to be oneself. The effects of antigay discrimination on the whole school community are also examined.

- Woog, Dan. *School's Out: The Impact of Gay and Lesbian Issues on American Schools.* Boston: Alyson Publications, 1995.

  A collection of nearly 300 interviews of gay men and lesbians and their heterosexual allies: students, teachers, principals, coaches, and counselors.

LGBT YOUTH SPEAK OUT

- Bass, Ellen and Kaufman, Kate. *Free Your Mind: The Book for Gay, Lesbian and Bisexual Youth and Their Allies.* New York: Harper Collins, 1996.

  A comprehensive guide for lesbian, gay, and bisexual teenagers, including ideas for how to make schools, Churches, and community organizations more open and affirming to gay teens.

- Chandler, Kurt. *Passages of Pride: Lesbian and Gay Youth Come of Age.* New York: Random House, 1995.

  A groundbreaking anthology of entertaining and affirming short stories geared especially for teenagers who are lesbian and gay or who have family and friends who are.

- Dane Bauer, Marion (Ed.). *Am I Blue? Coming Out From the Silence.* New York: Harper Collins, 1994.

  The stories of six lesbian and gay teens from Minnesota told in their own words. The book traces their journey from initial awareness, through self-disclosure and finding community. Compelling reading.

- Heron, Ann. *One Teenager in Ten: Writings by Gay and Lesbian Youth.* Boston: Alyson Publications, 1983.

  Lesbian and gay teenagers speak for themselves in this powerful and informative book.

PARENTS SPEAK OUT

- Borhek, Mary. *My Son Eric.* New York: Pilgrim Press, 1979.

  One mother's account of how she came to reconcile her son's homosexuality with her strong religious beliefs.

- Griffin, Carolyn W., Wirth, Marian J., and Wirth, Arthur J. *Beyond Acceptance: Parents of Lesbians and Gays Talk About Their Experiences.* New York: St. Martin's Press, 1986.

  Touching and illuminating stories of parents' struggles to come to terms with their lesbian and gay children and their own sense of family.

- McDougall, Bryce (Ed.). *My Child Is Gay: How Parents React When They Hear the News.* Australia: Allen & Unwin, 1998.

  A collection of honest and empowering stories about parents coming to terms with their children's sexuality.

THE LGBT REALITY AND THE CATHOLIC CHURCH

- Beattie Jung, Patricia. *Sexual Diversity and Catholicism: Toward the Development of Moral Theology.* Collegeville, MN: The Liturgical Press, 2001.

  Focusing specifically on Roman Catholic magisterial teachings, *Sexual Diversity and Catholicism* explores the mixed messages the Church sends about discrimination based on sexual identity. On the one hand, official documents have condemned violence and verbal abuse directed at persons of different sexual orientation; on the other hand, the Church has approved and lobbied for certain types of discrimination: in housing and employment, for example, and also with regard to marriage or civil unions. The book also examines the relationship among various sources of moral wisdom (Church teachings, the Bible, philosophy, science, and experience) and how their interplay might contribute to the further development of Church teaching.

- Coleman, Gerald D. *Homosexuality: Catholic Teaching and Pastoral Practice.* New York: Paulist Press, 1995.
- Liuzzi, Peter. *With Listening Hearts: Understanding the Voices of Lesbian and Gay Catholics.* New York: Paulist, 2001.

  Liuzzi, the Director of the Lesbian and Gay Ministry of the Archdiocese of Los Angeles and one of the leading figures in ministry to LGBT Catholics, presents a compassionate explanation of official Church teaching on homosexuality—including its limits. The book presents new, positive thoughts on the issue and the sound pastoral practices that arise from them. Above all, *With Listening Hearts* emphasizes the Church's position that personhood is more than one's sexual orientation and that the grace of God is found in every person and in his or her journey.

- New Ways Ministry. *Homosexuality: A Positive Catholic Perspective.* Mount Rainier: New Ways Ministry, 2003.

  A highly accessible and recommended question-and-answer-style booklet about gay and lesbian life and the teachings of the Catholic Church. Can be ordered from New Ways Ministry, 4012 29th St., Mt. Rainier, MD 20712 or by visiting www.newwaysministry.org.

THE LGBT REALITY AND THE CHRISTIAN CHURCH

- Boswell, John. *Christianity, Social Tolerance and Homosexuality.* Chicago: University of Chicago Press, 1980.

  A scholarly study that argues that the early Christian Church's position toward homosexuality was originally more sympathetic and only started to turn negative in the later Middle Ages. Some interesting, and what turned out to be academically controversial, ideas. Not for the casual reader.

- Comstock, Gary D. *Gay Theology Without Apology.* Cleveland: Pilgrim Press, 1993.

  A passionate and nonapologetic look at Christian theology as informed by Comstock's personal and spiritual experience as a gay man. Challenging to lesbian, gay, and straight reader alike.

- Countryman, William and Ritley, M.R. *Gifted by Otherness: Gay and Lesbian Christians in the Church.* Harrisburg: Morehouse Publishing, 2001.

  Proactive and affirming, *Gifted By Otherness* seeks to provide hope for those who feel that it is impossible to be gay or lesbian, as well as Christian. Basing their book on retreats they have presented to Churches and seminaries, the authors explore ways in which the gay and lesbian community can appropriate and retell the biblical story, and find confidence in their unique spiritual journey and gifts.

- Heyward, Carter. *Touching Our Strength: The Erotic as Power and the Love of God.* San Francisco: Harper and Row, 1989.
- Rudy, Kathy. *Sex and the Church: Gender, Homosexuality, and the Transformation of Christian Ethics.* Boston: Beacon Press, 1997.
- Stuart, Elizabeth. *Religion is a Queer Thing: A Guide to the Christian Faith for Lesbian, Gay, Bisexual and Transgendered People.* Cleveland: The Pilgrim Press, 1997.
- Waun, Maurine C. *More Than Welcome: Learning to Embrace Gay, Lesbian, Bisexual and Transgendered Persons in the Church.* St Louis: Chalice Press, 1999.

THE LGBT REALITY AND RELIGION

- Conner, Randy. *Blossom of Bone.* New York: Harper Collins Publishers, 1993.

A wide-ranging exploration of how gender-variant men have been involved in non-Christian religious systems across the world—from ancient times to the present. The book is helpful in seeing how religious traditions other than Christianity have often been more welcoming to men who love other men.

- Empereur, James L. *Spiritual Direction and the Gay Person.* New York: Continuum, 1999.

Robert Nugent, SDS., cofounder of New Ways Ministry, notes that *Spiritual Direction and the Gay Person* "is a first-class resource and guidebook for both spiritual directors and those in direction in the mutual journey to spiritual wholeness. Combining the best in contemporary personality development theory with a solid grasp of the central personal and social issues facing lesbian and gay people, the author provides a practical and balanced resource, even for the director approaching the subject for the first time."

- Swidler, Arlene (Ed.). *Homosexuality and World Religions.* Valley Forge, PA: Trinity Press, 1993.

A collection that provides detailed chapters on each of the major religions' responses to homosexuality—including the largely positive traditions of Native American peoples.

COMING OUT

- Borhek, Mary. *Coming Out to Parents: A Two-Way Survival Guide for Lesbians and Gay Men and Their Parents.* New York: Pilgrim Press, 1983.

A self-help guide for gay children and their parents. The book emerged in part out of Borhek's experiences after writing her first book, *My Son Eric.*

- de la Huerta, Christian. *Coming Out Spiritually: The Next Step.* New York: Jeremy P. Tarcher/ Putnam, 1999.

An examination of the ten spiritual roles or archetypes that LGBT people have often assumed and continue to enact today: creator of beauty, consciousness scout, mediator, shaman, and healer, among others. *Coming Out Spiritually* shows how to "look deeper inside; to reach higher than ever before; to step forth more fully into our rightful selves."

- Fairchild, Betty and Howard, Nancy. *Now That You Know: What Every Parent Should Know About Homosexuality.* New York: Harcourt, Brace, Jovanovich, 1990.

Probably the most popular and best first book to give to parents after coming out.

- Glaser, Chris. *Coming Out as Sacrament.* Louisville: Westminister John Know Press, 1998.
- Jensen, Karol L. *Lesbian Epiphanies: Women Coming Out in Later Life.* New York: Harrington Press, 1999.
- Johnson, Bret K. *Coming Out Every Day: A Gay, Bisexual, or Questioning Man's Guide.* Oakland: New Harbinger Publications, Inc., 1997.

Kate Kaufman, co-author of *Free Your Mind*, notes that *Coming Out Every Day* is "a useful, easy-to-read guidebook that uses narrative and exercises to coach gay, bisexual, and questioning men to greater self-awareness, self-acceptance, and ultimately to the ability to lead a more satisfying life."

- McCall Tigert, Leanne. *Coming Out While Staying In: Struggles and Celebrations of Lesbians, Gays, and Bisexuals in the Church.* Cleveland: United Church Press, 1996.
- Switzer, David K. *Coming Out As Parents: You and Your Homosexual Child.* Louisville, KT: Westminster John Knox Press, 1996.

CONFRONTING HETEROSEXISM AND HOMOPHOBIA

- Buchanan, Bob. *Love, Honor and Respect: How to Confront Homosexual Bias and Violence in Christian Culture.* Lincoln: Writers Club Press, 2000.
- McCall Tigert, Leanne. *Coming Out Through Fire: Surviving the Trauma of Homophobia.* Cleveland: United Church Press, 1999.

A book for GLBT persons who seek to move through the trauma of homophobia with the passion and power of transformation. It is also for pastors, therapists, and other helping professionals who seek to confront prejudice and fear and to further the process of healing and recovery in the Church and wider community.

- Morrison, Melanie. *The Grace of Coming Home: Spirituality, Sexuality, and the Struggle for Justice.* Cleveland: The Pilgrim Press, 1995.
- Sears, James T. and Williams, Walter L. *Overcoming Heterosexism and Homophobia: Strategies That Work.* New York: Columbia University Press.
- Sloan, Lacey M. and Gustavsson, Nora S. (Eds.). *Violence and Social Injustice Against Lesbian, Gay and Bisexual People.* Binghamton, NY: The Haworth Press, 1998.

Dorothy Van Soest, DSW, Associate Dean of the School of Social Work at the University of Texas, says that this book "exposes the multilevel nature of violence against gay, lesbian, bisexual, and transgendered people." She goes on to note the book "challenges the reader by illustrating multifaceted links between violence and injustice and analyzing root causes. By drawing attention to the intersectionality of multiple oppressions, the book's collection of articles illustrates how interpersonal, intrapersonal, and collective violence keeps diverse gay men and lesbians at the margin economically, politically, socially, and personally."

THE BIBLE AND HOMOSEXUALITY

- Horner, Tom. *Jonathan Loved David.* Philadelphia: Westminster Press, 1978.

Episcopalian priest Tom Horner explores various biblical passages—which have been used to condemn homosexuality—in their original historical and theological context.

- Scroggs, Robin. *The New Testament and Homosexuality.* Philadelphia: Fortress Press, 1983.

HUMAN SEXUALITY

- Baird, Vanessa. *The No-Nonsense Guide to Sexual Diversity.* Oxford: New Internationalist Publications Ltd., 2001.
- Isherwood, Lisa and Stuart, Elizabeth. *Introducing Body Theology.* Cleveland: The Pilgrim Press, 1998.

  Offers a body-centered theology that discusses cosmology, ecology, ethics, immortality, and sexuality, in a concise introduction that proposes and encourages a positive theology of the body.

- Nelson, James. *Embodiment.* Minneapolis: Augsburg Publishing, 1978.

  A groundbreaking book that takes an inclusive look at human sexuality and discusses a biblically grounded and ethical perspective that might guide the full expression of our humanity—straight or gay.

THE DIVERSITY OF LGBT EXPERIENCE

- Balka, Christine and Rose, Andy (Eds.). *Twice Blessed: On Being Lesbian, Gay and Jewish.* Boston: Beacon Press, 1989.

  Coming out and coming together stories from a Jewish perspective.

- Beam, J. *In the Life: A Black Gay Anthology.* Boston: Alyson Publishing, 1986.

  African Americans write about their experiences of coming out.

- Grever, C. *My Husband is Gay: A Woman's Guide to Surviving the Crisis.* Freedom: The Crossing Press, 2001.

  After thirty years of marriage, the author's husband told her he was gay. This disclosure led Grever on a five-year, soul-searching journey culminating in this book—which she describes as a road map for women in similar situations, and a survival kit for straight spouses.

- Williams, Walter L. *The Spirit and the Flesh: Sexual Diversity in American Indian Culture.* Boston: Beacon Press, 1986.

  A comprehensive look at the Native American tradition of the berdache, in history and at the present. The berdache is a gender-blending role with important implications for how we understand sexuality and culture, and how the two interact to shape our identities.

BISEXUALITY

- Hutchins L. and Kaahumani L. (Eds.). *Bi Any Other Name.* Boston: Alyson Publications, 1991.

  A collection of articles and essays exploring various issues and concerns of bisexual people.

- Kolodny, Debra R. (Ed.). *Blessed Bi Spirit: Bisexual People of Faith.* New York: Continuum, 2000.

  The first anthology in which bisexual persons speak for themselves. Reflecting a wide spectrum of religious traditions and spiritual paths, the thirty-two contributors speak about the intersections of their faith practice and their sexual orientation.

TRANSSEXUALITY

- Conover, P. *Transgender Good News.* Silver Spring, MD, 2002.

  In exploring various personal transgender journeys, *Transgender Good News* responds to three basic questions: What is true? What is going on? What really matters? A number of chapters focus on the religious implications of transgender expression and experience.

- Feinberg, Leslie. *Transgender Warriors: Making History from Joan of Arc to Dennis Rodman.* Boston: Beacon Press, 1996.

  The *San Francisco Chronicle Book Review* notes that *Transgender Warriors* "does far more than document the history of transgenders. It delves into the transgender experience, inviting the reader to consider a spectrum of gender possibilities."

- ————. *Trans Liberation: Beyond Pink or Blue.* Boston: Beacon Press, 1998.

  A collection of Feinberg's speeches on trans liberation and its essential connection to the liberation of all people.

- Mark Rees. *Dear Sir or Madam: The Autobiography of a Male-to-Female Transsexual.* London: Cassell, 1996.

INTERSEXUALITY

- Preves, Sharon E. *Intersex and Identity: The Contested Self.* New Brunswick: Rutgers University Press, 2003.

  A long overdue book that brings to life through interviews with adult intersexuals, the long-ignored voices of people who are born with a body that isn't simply male or female.

LGBT PEOPLE THROUGHOUT HISTORY AND AROUND THE WORLD

- Dynes, Wayne R. *Encyclopedia of Homosexuality.* New York: Garland Publishing, 1990.

  Massive two-volume hardcover encyclopedia that covers everything from homosexual life in Afghanistan to an essay on stereotypes—including over 150 abbreviated biographies of lesbian and gay figures throughout history.

- Grahn, Judy. *Another Mother Tongue.* Boston: Beacon Press, 1990 (revised edition).

  A beautiful book for anyone wanting to recapture a sense of their lesbian and gay heritage. Grahn, a poet, weaves myth and autobiography together—each strand amplifying the other.

- Heger, Heinz. *The Men with the Pink Triangles.* Boston: Alyson Publications, 1980.

  First-person account of a German homosexual who survived his imprisonment in the Nazi concentration camps. Contains a brief historical overview.

- Katz, Jonathan. *Gay American History.* New York: Thomas Y. Crowell, 1976.

Pioneering effort that collects obscure references to lesbian and gay lives from old newspapers, scholarly journals and travel records—dating back 350 years.

- Plant, Richard. *The Pink Triangle: The Nazi War Against Homosexuals.* New York: Henry Holt, 1986.

A chilling historical exploration of the status of homosexuals in German society prior to the rise of fascism, and the subsequent genocidal behavior of the Nazi regime. Plant's book provides the full historical context for Heger's personal memoir (see earlier).

- Richards, David A.J. *Identity and the Case for Gay Rights: Race, Gender, Religion as Analogies.* Chicago: The University of Chicago Press, 1999.

References

American Academy of Pediatrics (2002). Technical Report: Co-parent or Second Parent Adoption by Same-Sex Parents. *Pediatrics,* 109(2): 341-344.

American Psychological Association (1975). APA Policy Statement on Discrimination Against Homosexuals. Washington, DC: Author.

Augustine of Hippo (2001). *The Confessions of St. Augustine.* New York: Penguin Books.

Bailey, J.M. and Pillard, R. (1991). A Genetic Study of Male Sexual Orientation. *Archives of General Psychiatry,* 48, (December): 1089-1096.

Bailey, J.M. and Pillard, R. (1993). Heritable Factors Influence Sexual Orientation in Women. *Archives of General Psychiatry,* 50, (August): 217-223.

Bell, A.P., Weinberg, M.S., and Hammersmith, S.K. (1981). *Sexual Preference: Its Development in Men and Women.* Bloomington IN: Indiana University Press.

Benton County Sheriff's Office, Corvalis, Oregon

Blumenfeld, W.J. (1994). Adolescence, Sexual Orientation and Identity: An Overview. Published online from 1994-1998 by the Gay and Lesbian and Straight Education Network (GLSEN).

Catholic Pastoral Committee on Sexual Minorities (1999). Heterosexiam: Another Pillar of the Power Structure. Minneapolis: Author.

Catholic Pastoral Committee on Sexual Minorities (2003). An Official Statement Regarding Civil Marriage for Same-Gender Couples. Minneapolis: Author.

Catholic Social Welfare Commission of England and Wales (under Bishop Augustine Harris) (1978). *An Introduction to the Pastoral Care of Homosexual People.* London: Author.

Chase, A. (2001). Violent Reaction: What Do Teen Killers Have in Common? *In These Times,* July 9. pp. 16-18, 27. Available online: http://www.inthesetimes.com/issue/25/16/chase2516.html.

Congregation for Catholic Education (1983). *Educational Guidelines in Human Love.* Author.

Congregation for the Doctrine of the Faith (1986). *Letter to Bishops of the Catholic Church on the Pastoral Care of Homosexual Persons.* Author.

Congregation for the Doctrine of the Faith (2003). *Considerations Regarding Proposals to Give Legal Recognition to Unions Between Homosexual Persons.* Author.

Feder, F. and Heagle, J. (2002). *Tender Fire: The Spiritual Promises of Sexuality.* New York: Crossroad Press.

Fortunato, J. (1984). *Embracing the Exile.* SanFrancisco: Harper.

Gebhard, Paul H. and Johnson, Alan B. (1979). *The Kinsey Data: Marginal Tabulations of 1938-1963 Interviews Conducted by the Institute for Sex Research.* Bloomington, IN: Indiana University Press.

GLSEN. (2004). *Catholic School Facts from GLSEN's National School Climate Surveys.* New York: Author.

Groth, A.N. (1979). *Men Who Rape Men.* New York: Plenum Press.

Gumbleton, T.J. (2001). Teaching Authentically. *America: The National Catholic Weekly,* 184 (14).

Helminiak, D. (2006). A New Way of Envisioning Wholeness. *Rainbow Spirit,* 8(1): 11, 18-19.

Herbert, (Ed.) (1969). *Gaudium et Spes* (The church in the modern world). In Burns and Oats, Commentary on the Documents of Vatican II, Vorgrinler (p.134).

Hower, J.A., Bankins, M., and Crahen, S. (1987). Appreciation of Difference: Riddle Scale of Homophobia. Paper presented at the meeting of ACPA/NASPA Celebration, Chicago.

Kinsey, A. et al. (1948). *Sexual Behavior in the Human Male.* Philadelphia: W.B. Saunders Co.

Kinsey, A. et al. (1953). *Sexual Behavior in the Human Female.* Philadelphia: Saunders.

Kosciw, J.G. (2004). *The 2003 National School Climate Survey: The School-Related Experiences of Our Nation's Lesbian, Gay,Bisexual and Transgender Youth.* New York: GLSEN.

Kosciw, J.G. and Cullen, M.K. (2002). *The 2001 National School Climate Survey: The School-Related Experiences of Our Nation's Lesbian, Gay, Bisexual and Transgender Youth.* New York: GLSEN.

LeVay, S. (1991). A Difference in Hypothalamic Structure Between Heterosexual and Homosexual Men. *Science,* 253: 1034-1037.

Libreria Editrice Vaticana (1997). *Catechism of the Catholic Church.* Author.

Creating Safe Environments for LGBT Students
© 2007 by The Haworth Press, Inc. All rights reserved.
doi:10.1300/5723_11

Norris, K. (2001). *Dakota: A Spiritual Geography.* Mariner Books. p. 69.

Ojeda, A. (Ed.) (2003). *Homosexuality: Opposing Viewpoints.* San Diego: Greenhaven Press.

O'Leary, J. (1998). Mother Church and Her Gay/Lesbian Children. *Ceide.* September/October.

Quinn, J. (1987). Toward an Understanding of the Letter on the Pastoral Care of Homosexual Persons. *America: The National Catholic Weekly,* 184 (14): 92-116.

Reis, B. and Saewyc, E. (1999). Seattle Schools' 1995 Youth Risk Behavior Survey. In *Eighty-Three Thousand Youth: Selected Findings of Eight Population-based Studies.* Safe Schools Coalition of Washington (Ed.).

Rich, A. (1994). *Blood, Bread, and Poetry.* New York: Norton.

Roach, John R. (1991). A Statement on Homosexual Persons and the Protection of Human Rights. *The Catholic Bulletin,* September 26.

Rowson, E. (1991). The Categorization of Gender and Sexual Irregularity in Medieval Arabic Vise Lists. In J. Epstein and K. Straub (Eds.) *Body Guards: The Cultural Products of Ambiguity* (p. 73). New York and London: Routledge.

Russell, S. and Joyner, K. (2001). Adolescent Sexual Orientation and Suicide Risk: Evidence from a National Study. *American Journal of Public Health,* 91(8): 1276-1281. Available online http://www.pubmedcentral.nih.gov.

Ryan, C. and Futterman, D. (1998). *Gay Youth: Care and Counseling.* New York: Columbia.

Second Vatican Council (1965). *Declaration on Christian Education.* Author.

U.S. Census Bureau. Current Population Survey. Author.

U.S. Conference of Catholic Bishops (1973). *Principles to Guide Confessors.* Author.

U.S. Conference of Catholic Bishops (1976). *To Live in Jesus.* Author.

U. S. Conference of Catholic Bishops (1979). *National Catechetical Directory.* Author.

U.S. Conference of Catholic Bishops (1981). *Education in Human Sexuality for Christians.* Author.

U.S. Conference of Catholic Bishops (1990). *Human Sexuality: A Catholic Perspective for Education and Lifelong Learning.* Author.

U.S. National Conference of Catholic Bishops (1997). *Always Our Children: A Pastoral Message to Parents of Homosexual Children and Suggestions for Pastoral Ministers.* Author.

Weakland, R. (1980). *The Catholic Herald,* July 19.

Index

(boldface indicates handout sample)

Order a copy of this book with this form or online at:
http://www.haworthpress.com/store/product.asp?sku=5723

CREATING SAFE ENVIRONMENTS FOR LGBT STUDENTS
A Catholic Schools Perspective

_____in softbound at $17.95 (ISBN: 978-1-56023-606-1)

145 pages plus index • Includes illustrations

Or order online and use special offer code HEC25 in the shopping cart.

COST OF BOOKS_____

☐ **BILL ME LATER:** (Bill-me option is good on US/Canada/Mexico orders only; not good to jobbers, wholesalers, or subscription agencies.)

☐ Check here if billing address is different from shipping address and attach purchase order and billing address information.

POSTAGE & HANDLING_____
(US: $4.00 for first book & $1.50 for each additional book)
(Outside US: $5.00 for first book & $2.00 for each additional book)

Signature_____

SUBTOTAL_____

☐ **PAYMENT ENCLOSED:** $_____

IN CANADA: ADD 6% GST_____

☐ **PLEASE CHARGE TO MY CREDIT CARD.**

STATE TAX_____
(NJ, NY, OH, MN, CA, IL, IN, PA, & SD residents, add appropriate local sales tax)

☐ Visa ☐ MasterCard ☐ AmEx ☐ Discover
☐ Diner's Club ☐ Eurocard ☐ JCB

Account # _____

FINAL TOTAL_____
(If paying in Canadian funds, convert using the current exchange rate, UNESCO coupons welcome)

Exp. Date_____

Signature_____

Prices in US dollars and subject to change without notice.

NAME_____

INSTITUTION_____

ADDRESS_____

CITY_____

STATE/ZIP_____

COUNTRY_____ COUNTY (NY residents only)_____

TEL_____ FAX_____

E-MAIL_____

May we use your e-mail address for confirmations and other types of information? ☐ Yes ☐ No
We appreciate receiving your e-mail address and fax number. Haworth would like to e-mail or fax special discount offers to you, as a preferred customer. **We will never share, rent, or exchange your e-mail address or fax number.** We regard such actions as an invasion of your privacy.

Order From Your Local Bookstore or Directly From
The Haworth Press, Inc.
10 Alice Street, Binghamton, New York 13904-1580 • USA
TELEPHONE: 1-800-HAWORTH (1-800-429-6784) / Outside US/Canada: (607) 722-5857
FAX: 1-800-895-0582 / Outside US/Canada: (607) 771-0012
E-mail to: orders@haworthpress.com

For orders outside US and Canada, you may wish to order through your local sales representative, distributor, or bookseller.
For information, see http://haworthpress.com/distributors

(Discounts are available for individual orders in US and Canada only, not booksellers/distributors.)

PLEASE PHOTOCOPY THIS FORM FOR YOUR PERSONAL USE.
http://www.HaworthPress.com   BOF07

Dear Customer:

Please fill out & return this form to receive special deals & publishing opportunities for you! These include:
- availability of new books in your local bookstore or online
- one-time prepublication discounts
- free or heavily discounted related titles
- free samples of related Haworth Press periodicals
- publishing opportunities in our periodicals or Book Division

❑ OK! Please keep me on your regular mailing list and/or e-mailing list for new announcements!

Name _____

Address_____

_____

*E-mail address _____
*Your e-mail address will never be rented, shared, exchanged, sold, or divested. You may "opt-out" at any time.
May we use your e-mail address for confirmations and other types of information? ❑ Yes ❑ No

Special needs:
Describe below any special information you would like:
- Forthcoming professional/textbooks
- New popular books
- Publishing opportunities in academic periodicals
- Free samples of periodicals in my area(s)

Special needs/Special areas of interest:

_____

_____

_____

_____

Please contact me as soon as possible. I have a special requirement/project:

_____

_____

_____

_____

PLEASE COMPLETE THE FORM ABOVE AND MAIL TO:
Donna Barnes, Marketing Dept., The Haworth Press, Inc.
10 Alice Street, Binghamton, NY 13904–1580 USA
Tel: 1–800–429–6784 • Outside US/Canada Tel: (607) 722–5857
Fax: 1–800–895–0582 • Outside US/Canada Fax: (607) 771–0012
E-mail: orders@HaworthPress.com

GBIC07

Visit our Web site: www.HaworthPress.com